THE MURDER OF LACI PETERSON

The inside story of what really happened

BY CLIFF LINEDECKER

Edited by Nicholas Maier

American Media, Inc.

THE MURDER OF LACI PETERSON
The Inside Story of What Really Happened

Copyright © 2003 AMI Books, Inc.

Cover design: Carlos Plaza
Interior design: Debbie Browning

ISBN: 1-932270-17-5

First printing: July 2003

Printed in the United States of America

10 9 8 7 6 5 4 3 2 1

ACKNOWLEDGEMENTS

The following *National Enquirer* reporters deserve special mention for their tireless investigative efforts on the Laci Peterson murder story and their contributions to this book: Michelle Caruso, Don Gentile, Mike Hanrahan, Charlie Montgomery, Jim Nelson, John South and David Wright.

AUTHOR'S NOTE

In the United States all suspects are innocent until proven guilty by a court of law. Certain events in this book have been recreated from evidence uncovered by our reporters.

PROLOGUE

Homicide is the leading cause of death for pregnant women in America.

This shocking statistic was issued in a 2001 report released by the American Medical Association, which disclosed that a time typically reserved for the celebration of life often sets the stage for murder. According to the study, an expectant mother is less likely to succumb to a medical complication such as an embolism or hemorrhaging than to be killed by a husband or lover.

Police records show that this trend cut across all races and socioeconomic classes, and many of the abusers were educated, upstanding citizens prior to snapping. In some cases, the women were beaten for years and the violence escalated after they became pregnant. In others, the pregnancy itself sparked emotions that led to rages by their partner. Psychologists believe that these men suddenly feel trapped in a relationship where they are no longer the center of attention, leading to the homicidal violence.

Using death records and coroner reports, state health department researchers in Maryland found 247 pregnancy-associated deaths between 1993 and 1998, including 50 that were homicides. In Chicago's Cook County, Illinois, 26 percent of the 95 deaths of pregnant women recorded between 1986 and 1989 were homicides. And in New York, 25 percent of the 293 deaths among pregnant women between 1987 and 1991 were also related to intentional acts of violence.

For most women and men alike, the birth of a new baby is considered a miracle. A child represents all the dreams and hopes each one of us hold dear. But for those unlucky few that never imagined they might be added to these grim statistics, that same miracle led to murder.

INTRODUCTION

Glittering Christmas lights were strung on porches and in yards at neighboring homes all around the tidy three-bedroom green clapboard ranch home at 523 Covena Avenue in Modesto when Laci and Scott Peterson stepped outside and climbed into her Range Rover SUV for the short drive into town to the Salon Salon.

While her husband had his hair shaped and trimmed for the holiday by Laci's half-sister, 21-year-old Amy Rocha, the two young women exchanged casual small talk. Even though the sisters enjoyed and looked forward to their beauty parlor chitchat, Scott typically spent more time there than his wife did. The handsome, powerfully built golfer and outdoorsman was vain about his looks and a regular client at Salon Salon. Although 30 years old, if Scott spotted a single hair that had faded from its natural dark brown to any shade even remotely approaching gray he made sure that it was immediately dyed back to the original color. He could afford to stay well-groomed — Amy didn't charge him or her sister for her services.

Laci possessed her own eye-catching good looks, but the 5-foot-1-inch 27-year-old woman's normally petite body was swollen with the late stages of pregnancy. Her focus at that time wasn't on beauty, but on the birth of her child that was only a few weeks away. While Amy snipped and clipped, the sisters carried on about the baby and the holidays until Scott meticulously inspected his hair in the mirrors, decided it looked satisfactory, slid out of his chair and got up to leave.

The couple ran a few more errands before returning to the house, where they puttered around with chores, watched some television and finally sat down to their dinner.

About 8:30 p.m. on Dec. 23, Laci dialed her mother, Sharon Rocha, who lived in Modesto with her second husband, Ron Grantski. The women chatted on the telephone for a few minutes and Laci confirmed to her mother that she and Scott would be at the their home at 6 p.m. on Christmas Eve to share a festive family dinner. When Laci ...ded the conversation to get ready for bed and change into her nightclothes, it marked the last time the mother and daughter would ever talk.

The enthusiastic mother-to-be would never be seen by anyone in the Grantski or Rocha families again. When Laci hung up the telephone that night, investigators believe, she had only minutes left to live.

Chapter 1

LACI

One of the first things that Sharon Rocha noticed about the baby girl the maternity ward nurse placed in her arms was the conspicuously deep dimples in her cheeks. The new mother recognized the feature as a sign that the tiny infant would be a happy baby with a vibrant, sunny personality and she was right on target.

From the day of her birth at Doctor's Medical Center in Modesto, California, on May 4, 1975, Laci Denise Rocha was a contented child. Within a few days, she was sleeping through the night with no noisy interruptions, her mother told the local newspaper, the *Modesto Bee*. And whenever the proud mom prepared to lift her out of her crib, the baby awakened with a smile.

Laci grew up devoted to her family, enthusiastic and excited by the challenges and rewards of life and, for the most part, lived a golden childhood. Her parents owned a 40-acre dairy farm just outside the flyspeck country town of Escalon, about 10 miles north of Modesto, a charming northern California city of just under 200,000, in the lush San Joaquin Valley. Municipal leaders were so proud of Modesto, with its almond trees, nearby strawberry fields and dairy farms, that they erected a sign on the main highway leading into town with the slogan, "Water, Wealth, Contentment, Health." The little girl blossomed, living the healthy, outdoor life and was barely bigger than a wood sprite when she began climbing into a pair of her father Dennis Rocha's big rubber boots and clumsily trailing behind him while he was busy with chores.

By the time Laci was 5 years old, her mother says she realized she had "a little flower girl" on her hands. One day, Sharon brought home a new weed puller and her daughter insisted on going outside to try it out. Laci quickly learned to tell the difference between weeds and more appreciated greenery such as flowers and vegetables. She loved to play in the dirt and, according to the *Modesto Bee*, was always asking her mother: "Can I go pull the weeds?"

Laci was already showing signs of what would become a lifelong attraction to growing things and gardening became a passion. Even when inside the house, she was often watering, trimming or otherwise fussing with plants.

Throughout those early years, Laci adored her older brother Brent and followed him around like a shadow. Like most children who grow up on farms, they couldn't play with the kids next door because the nearest neighbors lived a considerable distance away. So, despite the gap in ages — Brent was four years older — the siblings spent much of their time playing together. The kids made their own fun.

One day during a family gathering, Laci and about 20 people were gathered around the pool when Brent dared her to peel off her bathing suit and jump in. She did and then scrambled out as her horrified grandmother rushed up to cover her with a towel. "Now, honey, when people are around you have to keep your suit on," the grandmother admonished.

"It was Brent's fault," the irrepressible 5-year-old responded. "He dared me!"

Like most kids who are raised on dairy farms, the Rocha siblings were expected to carry their share of the workload on the farm, with responsibilities that increased as they grew older and stronger. There were always cows to be milked, fed and cleaned up after, as well as other chores to take care of in the barn, pastures, fields and house.

Growing up on a dairy farm was always an adventure and the siblings learned early to look down at the ground when they were walking around, especially when they were barefoot, to make sure they didn't step into a cow plop or anything equally unpleasant. But one day as they were trying to cross an ocean of mud and manure, Laci got into serious trouble, Brent later told the *Modesto Bee*.

She was wearing boots that were too big for her feet, and when they got stuck she tumbled smack down into the slimy mess. Her arms were sinking in the sticky muck while she screamed and yelled for help. Farmhands were working nearby and instead of running to the rescue they broke up into roars of laughter.

Laci was understandably angry at first, but in moments she realized how ridiculous the situation was that she had gotten herself into. Her familiar, big dimpled smile began to spread across her face and in moments she was also howling with laughter.

It wasn't long before Laci was driving her family's tractor by herself, scooting to the edge of the seat, hanging onto the steering wheel and stretching her skinny little legs to reach the pedals. She loved animals, had a dog and learned to ride horses. Growing up on a farm was paradise for the little girl and as the old saying goes, "life was a bowl of cherries."

But almost no one, no matter how lucky, moves through life without a few rough tumbles and when Laci was 7 years old her parents divorced. Sharon retained custody of her two kids. The children were already close and the divorce made them even closer. Laci was a daddy's girl and both parents worked extra hard to make sure that she continued to spend lots of quality time with her adoring father at the farm.

Another bump in the road came when Laci was 8 years old. When an ovary became infected, she had to undergo surgery to have the organ removed. In typical fashion, Laci recovered quickly and went on with life all the more content to have made it through the medical emergency.

When Laci's mother married Ron Grantski, he moved smoothly into the role of substitute dad to his stepchildren and developed a loving father-and-daughter relationship with the bright, brown-eyed little girl. Because Sharon's two children were Rochas, the mother continued to use her former husband's name. At about that time, Laci also became a big sister when Dennis Rocha and his new wife became parents of a daughter. They named the little girl Amy.

Laci was a tiny child, smaller than many of her friends at school, but she made up in spirit what she lacked in size and kept right up with her peers when it came to organized athletics. When she was 6 years old and attended the Sonoma Elementary School, she played in the Modesto Girls Softball Association.

After Sonoma, Laci attended La Loma Junior High School and then moved on to Downey High, where she was as a cheer-leader. As she became a beautiful teenager, all of Brent's friends began to pay more attention to his sister, he later recalled to the *Modesto Bee*. They would say things like, "Man, your sister is really cute." Brent began to respond to her suggestions that she hang out with him and the guys by telling her that he didn't think that was such a good idea. That was OK — the carefree girl with the sunny disposition never had trouble making friends.

By that time the bubbly teenager's stepfather had adopted a special nickname for her — "Jabber Jaws" — because she loved to talk and could always be counted on to be the life of the party. She did a lot of her jabbering with a special circle of chums, some who had been among her best friends since Sonoma Elementary School. Like Laci, a few of the girls were cheerleaders, others played softball and different sports, but they all hung out together, partied together and faithfully supported the Downey High football squad at games.

The group gossiped about the school jocks and other boys at slumber parties while demolishing scads of pizzas and soda pop. Sometimes they sneaked champagne into the bedroom past unsuspecting parents. That often meant hangovers for just about everybody, but Laci always made it to school the next day. The girls especially liked sleeping over at Staci Western's house because her mother slept so deeply that they could slip out on the town once she nodded off.

Even on the slightly woozy post-champagne mornings, there was no doubt that Laci was a true beauty when decked out in her blue-and-white cheerleader's uniform with her shoulder-length dark hair and exotic café au lait complexion. Her charm could make the high school boys self-consciously scramble for their words while struggling to remember their own names.

Laci was one of the most popular girls at school, her pal Melinda Freeman, who met her at Downey High, later recalled. "But she wasn't flirty and only dated a few guys." That wasn't because the guys didn't ask. Even at that age, Laci was confidently discriminating and had a firm idea of what she wanted and expected in a boyfriend.

In 1993, after graduation from high school, Laci enrolled at California Polytechnic State University in San Luis Obispo, where she majored in ornamental horticulture. She couldn't have picked a more appropriate subject, and her love for plants and her natural ability — honed throughout her childhood by spending hours in the flower and vegetable gardens back in Modesto — quickly paid off.

After her first year of classes at Cal Poly, Laci walked away with the outstanding freshmen award in ornamental horticulture. She also demonstrated her skills in flower judging and as a member of Cal Poly's landscape team in competition with other horticulture schools around the country and she belonged to Pi Alpha Xi, the horticulture honor society. Soon enough, she became the manager of the college's plant shop.

Her big brother was impressed when he drove to the campus to visit, according to the *Modesto Bee*. Instead of hauling him off to some frat house for keg parties, she took Brent to wine tastings at area wineries. She already knew all the rules, like starting out with the whites and working your way through the reds.

By 1995, Laci had settled into an apartment in the nearby oceanside town of Morro Bay. The communities strung along the shoreline of the Pacific were charming and wonderful places to live. Laci loved being a college coed and she was looking forward to spreading her wings and meeting whatever challenges the future had in store for her.

Chapter 2

SCOTT

The son of parents who ran their own successful business, Scott Peterson grew up as the baby of a large family that included two girls and five boys. Born at Sharp Hospital in San Diego on Oct. 24, 1971, Scott's mother told the *Modesto Bee* that she remembered him as a healthy, happy baby.

Lee and Jacqueline "Jackie" Peterson were loving and protective parents who raised their brood in Solano Beach, a wealthy enclave of homes near San Diego. Compared to many children, especially in such large families, Scott was a privileged child and like his older brothers, was barely out of diapers before his father began passing on his love of golf, fishing and hunting to the last of the Peterson boys.

At first, fishing took precedence over golf, but by the time Scott was 6 years old he had learned to combine the two. His parents frequently gathered up the family for outings at a golf course on the San Diego River and the little boy always made sure to store a fishing pole in his golf bag alongside his mini-clubs.

Years later, his mother recalled to the *Bee* that by the time they were ready to tee up on the second hole, Scott would pull out his fishing pole and head for the river. He would fish until the rest of the family finished with their golf game.

Lee Peterson also took his boys on frequent fishing trips to the mountains and it was Scott who eventually talked him into buying a boat. But the Petersons didn't give up on making a golfer out of their youngest son and they eventually succeeded in sparking his interest by allowing him to drive the golf cart while they were on the links.

Scott began to take the sport more seriously and by the time he was a student at the University of San Diego High School, he played on the varsity golf team from 1987 to

1990 and was twice named most valuable player. During three of his four years in high school, Scott made the *San Diego Tribune*'s All-Academic Team.

Scott's father once promised him that if he ever played a round of scratch golf, he would buy him a Ferrari. He astounded his parents by shooting par while still in high school. He didn't get the Ferrari because they worried that the sleek little speedster would be too dangerous for a teenage boy, so they bought him a used Peugeot sedan, according to the *Modesto Bee*.

Some people may have considered Scott outrageously spoiled, but he wasn't lazy and somehow amid all the good times — the fishing, the hunting and the play — he became handy with tools. He was good at fixing things up.

There was no getting around it, however, that Scott was at his confident best when he had a fishing pole or a golf club in his hands. He was the star of the University of San Diego High School varsity golf team and he knew he was the star. According to some of his former classmates, he went to great lengths to make sure other people knew it, as well. His swaggering self-assurance could be a turnoff. At times he came across as a cocky braggart or an insufferable snob. What some people around Scott saw as an engaging smile, others saw as a condescending smirk.

Scott "was a tremendous kid and a tremendous golfer," recalled Dave Thoennes, who coached him during all four years he was on the high school team. "He was popular and a leader."

Thoennes described Scott as a natural athlete who developed into a leader during his sophomore year after teammate Phil Mickelson graduated. After playing his freshman year alongside Mickelson, who turned professional and now tours with the PGA, Scott became the anchor for teams that competed in regional and state tournaments.

Thoennes remembered Scott as a player who was never late for practice and a boy who was dependable, disciplined and had a great personality.

Not everyone who knew Scott or played with him on the golf team agreed with that — or with his mother's glowing recollections of her youngest son. Some of his schoolmates and teammates considered him to be a jerk and a prima donna.

Ed Ventura said that Scott was a snob who continually boasted about how good he played and how much better he was than his peers on the links. Scott could always be depended on to help the team and other members of the squad wanted him to play, but no one wanted to be around him after the competition ended, his former teammate recalled. "He was a loner. At school he was the kind of guy you would walk by and not even notice."

Although some of his classmates and peers later remembered him as conceited and arrogant, there was another, more appealing side to the teenager. When the occasion called for it, or if he was in the mood, Scott could be charming.

None of his grandparents were living and somehow he befriended an elderly woman with no grandchildren. He went out of his way to visit her on Sundays after church. Scott's high school encouraged community service and one time he took his adopted grandmother to class with him on Grandparents' Day.

Scott's mother later recalled her surprise when her son told her about his plan, prompting her to ask, "Where did you get a grandmother?"

He replied simply that he had one for a while.

According to the *Modesto Bee*, Jackie Peterson went with her son the following

Sunday to meet his adopted grandparent and the woman went on and on about what a nice boy he was to visit an old lady.

In recalling other examples of Scott's warm heart and kindness, Mrs. Peterson said she and her husband also received a couple of letters from strangers who were helped by Scott after their cars broke down on the road.

When Scott graduated from high school in 1990, his ability on the links was good enough to earn him a partial golf scholarship at Arizona State University. He only stayed there for six months, leaving to return home when his family moved into a house they bought in the charming oceanside town of Morro Bay, about midway between San Francisco and Los Angeles.

That arrangement didn't last long, either. The husky, athletic young man soon came to the conclusion that he was too old to still be living with his parents and he moved out on his own. He worked three jobs to pay the bills for studies at Cuesta College and California Polytechnic State University in nearby San Luis Obispo, where he majored in agriculture.

Scott was working at one of those jobs, waiting tables at the Pacific Café in the summer of 1994, when he met a vibrant coed with a winsome smile that stretched from deep dimple to deep dimple on her cheeks. For Laci Denise Rocha, it was love at first sight.

Chapter 3

PRINCE CHARMING

Sharon Rocha immediately recognized the voice of her oldest daughter when she walked into the living room and picked up the receiver of the ringing telephone — but the message was a bit of a surprise.

"Mother, I have met the man I am going to marry," Laci enthusiastically bubbled. "You've just got to get down here and meet him."

Mrs. Rocha told the *Modesto Bee* that she asked her 19-year-old daughter if she and the young man she was so excited about had dated.

"Not yet," Laci confidently replied, "but we will."

One of her neighbors worked at the Pacific Café and Laci often dropped by to sip coffee and chat. One of the other employees she paid the most attention to was a handsome, athletically built waiter named Scott Peterson. He was a charmer, with a ready line of patter. He seemed to be as comfortable with women as he obviously was with himself. Like Laci, Scott was an undergraduate at Cal Poly.

After they had talked a few times and he still hadn't asked for a date, the 19-year-old coed took matters in her own hands. She scribbled her telephone number on a slip of paper and asked her neighbor to give it to Scott at work.

Scott thought he was being set up for a nasty practical joke when he took the paper and peered at the phone number, so he crumpled it up and dropped it in the trash. But after Scott's co-worker convinced him the pretty young woman really was interested in a date, he rummaged around in the garbage bin, dug it out and gave Laci a call.

When they met for their first date that week, Scott took Laci on a deep-sea fishing trip, according to the *Modesto Bee*. She was anxious to make a good impression on the handsome hunk she had just reeled in, but she grew up amid the dairy farms, strawberry fields and almond orchards of the San Joaquin Valley, not the scatter of communities along the shoreline of the Pacific Ocean. They were barely at sea before she began feeling woozy and she became violently seasick.

If she worried that her seasickness would spell disaster for the budding romance, she was wrong. Scott probably figured there would be plenty of time later for the girl from Modesto to develop sea legs. Or perhaps she was exactly what she appeared to be — a satin, lace and red roses type of girl who was never cut out for roughing it in choppy seas three or four miles from land. Whatever his reasoning, Scott and Laci quickly became an item.

Sharon Rocha had promised to drive down to Morro Bay and take a look at her daughter's Prince Charming for herself and the meeting wasn't a disappointment. Scott was at his engaging best. He pulled out all the stops in efforts to favorably impress his girlfriend's mother.

Scott warmly greeted mother and daughter at the front door of the restaurant, according to the *Modesto Bee*, and told Sharon what a pleasure it was to meet her. Then, still smiling broadly, he turned to Laci and advised: "Ma'am, I have your favorite table waiting for you."

So many roses were arranged in vases on the table that it looked like there would hardly be any room for food. Scott had selected 12 white roses for his girlfriend's mother and 12 red roses for Laci.

The young man seemed the perfect gentleman and Sharon was impressed. Even more, she could tell her daughter was head-over-heels in love.

Laci later confided to a girlfriend that Scott was everything she wanted in a man — gentle, athletic, handsome and very ambitious.

Scott was equally entranced and a few weeks after he and Laci began dating, he took her home to San Diego to show her off to his family. It seemed to his parents and the other Peterson kids that their little brother simply couldn't stop smiling.

The couple dated nearly three years before tying the knot while they were still in college. Laci was giving up her lifelong dream of becoming a professional horticulturalist to realize another dream — marrying the perfect man. Her parents recalled that from that point on, she focused wholeheartedly on being there for Scott.

Aug. 9, 1997, was Laci's wedding day, a time that young lovers reserve solely for the celebration of life. The lovely 22-year-old bride's thoughts were filled with the promise of children yet-to-be conceived and her handsome husband's everlasting love.

"It was a beautiful wedding, small and very private," Heather Richardson, Laci's closest friend and maid of honor, recalled. Heather's husband, Mike, was best man.

The picture-perfect setting for her wedding was just as Laci had always dreamed. The afternoon sun streamed through the slatted roof of the romantic gazebo at Sycamore Mineral Springs Resort, casting a delicate shadow upon a three-tiered wedding cake festooned with clusters of pink and white roses. Pink and white were Laci's signature colors.

Tucked away on a wooded hillside, the San Luis Obispo resort has been a popular location for weddings and receptions since the late 1890s. Laci fell in love with the resort when she worked there and became convinced that the resort's gazebo gardens were the most romantic spot in America.

On her wedding day, Laci was resplendent in a white satin wedding gown and train with a halter-style lace bodice. Her upswept hairdo — set off by diamond earrings — was adorned with a delicate lace headband and flowing veil. As she walked to the altar, she carried a magnificent cascading bouquet of pink and white roses.

Laci's father, Dennis Rocha, was supposed to walk her down the aisle and give her away. But he was working at his ranch earlier in the day and arrived just minutes before the ceremony, so Dennis' dad stepped in and performed the honors.

"I was late for the ceremony, so my father walked Laci down the aisle," he later explained. "Laci was very close to her grandfather, so she was happy he was there for her."

The petite, glowing bride was met at the altar by her beaming 25-year-old fiancé, Scott, who towered over her. He looked like a storybook prince in white tie and tails, with a white rose boutonniere pinned to his waistcoat lapel as they promised to love and to hold each other "until death do us part."

Photographer Patti Sala shot the wedding

pictures and later recalled: "They looked like the perfect couple who had everything to live for. Laci was one of the most beautiful brides I'd ever seen. She was stunning and didn't stop smiling the whole time. You could tell she was looking forward to spending the rest of her life with Scott. She looked at him like she would do absolutely anything for him — anything!"

Chapter 4

MR. & MRS.

As the happy couple settled into married life, they still had college bills to pay, so they drew on Scott's experience in restaurants to establish their own business — a hamburger joint a few minutes walk from the Cal Poly campus that they named The Shack.

The Shack was a bakery before Laci and Scott converted it into a restaurant and they lined the walls with television sets tuned to sporting events and decorated the dining area with barrels filled with peanuts in the shell. The idea was for everyone to help themselves to all the peanuts they wanted to eat and then drop the crushed shells onto the floor. The atmosphere was casual, the food was good and they were in an excellent location. Their customers included college students, surfers, beach bums and thousands of others who either lived or vacationed in the area.

The restaurant paid most of the bills, but the couple was young and liked to live well, so late in 2000 they declared bankruptcy, even though they were only $5,000 in debt. They had decided to pull up stakes and return to Laci's hometown, Modesto, where she had high hopes of getting pregnant so she could achieve her heart's desire and raise a family of happy kids.

In Modesto, Laci was delighted to be back among her chums from high school once again. The young women — some married and some not — quickly rekindled their old friendships. Laci brought the old gang back together and they even had a few sleepovers that led to gossiping until light began to show in the pre-dawn sky and birds began to stir and peep outside.

The move to Modesto also meant Laci was securely snuggled back among her family, and she could replace phone calls with personal visits whenever the couple felt like climbing into a car for a few minutes drive across town or into the country to her father's dairy farm.

Scott landed a new job as a salesman for Tradecorp, a specialty fertilizer company with a home base in Madrid, Spain, that distributes its product worldwide. He became the company's representative for all of California and the neighboring state of Arizona. His responsibilities included handling the wholesale end of the business and marketing the company's fertilizer to retail businesses.

Despite the less than romantic product he sold, the job offered enormous potential for an ambitious young go-getter like Scott. That was especially true in Modesto and the surrounding communities and farmland of the San Joaquin Valley in the middle of California's breadbasket. Agriculture is a $15 billion business — the No. 1 industry — in the lush Valley, so it may have appeared to outsiders that all Scott had to do to become a rousing success was show up for work. But the business of hawking fertilizer for a chemical industry that is constantly coming out with new products was brutally competitive and Scott, along with hundreds of other salesmen, had to work hard to convince cautious retailers to buy their fertilizer.

Tradecorp maintained a strong sales presence in countries such as France, Turkey, Chile and South Africa. But although the company heavily targeted orchards like those that dotted the Valley landscape and other areas of the state, their fertilizers were carried by only a small percentage of retailers in California. It was Scott's job to help change that. The task was especially challenging because Scott was pitching premium fertilizers and minerals with higher prices than many of his competitors at a time when the agriculture business was coping with a tight farm economy.

While Scott was beating the bushes to sell fertilizer, Laci snagged a job with the local school system as a substitute teacher. It was a good career choice. Even though it wasn't horticulture, she would still be working with growing things — except that instead of nurturing plants she would be nurturing kids. She wasn't much bigger than some of them, but it was her enthusiastic personality and natural mothering instincts that helped her keep the students' attention.

For a while, Laci and Scott rented a small place in the area. Then they found the perfect home — a fixer-upper at 523 Covena

Avenue in Modesto's La Loma neighborhood that was available for $177,000. The home came with a garage that had been converted into a family room. They made a down payment, then took out a mortgage for $141,600 in October 2000 and moved in.

The neighborhood was near East La Loma Park, one of a string of smaller woodlands that made up the larger Dry Creek Park. East La Loma Park was where Laci walked her dog, McKenzie, a beautiful and high-spirited golden retriever.

The clapboard house offered a perfect opportunity for Scott to show off his self-acquired skills with tools. He remodeled the entire place, doing much of the work himself, including woodworking, laying tile, even plumbing. But he hired a contractor when the couple decided they needed a swimming pool and professionals installed the new air conditioning system.

The house was big, with three bedrooms, two baths and plenty of extra room. Even though after several years of marriage there was still no sign that a baby might be on the way, Scott remodeled one of the bedrooms into a nursery — just in case.

Laci dearly wanted a baby, but her childhood loss of an ovary made it difficult for her to conceive and she wasn't sure if she would ever be successful in her desire to become a mom. Although Scott also talked about a desire to become a parent, the couple decided to let nature take its course and didn't seek fertility treatments or other medical help to boost Laci's chances of conception.

As a part-time employee with the school system, she had the opportunity to tend to some of her other favorite activities, beginning with homemaking. She selected elegant furnishings and personal touches were evident everywhere, from the plants and flowers inside to the shrubs and greenery that she so lovingly cared for outside.

The couple tended a vegetable garden in their backyard and every so often neighbors would hear a knock on the door and find either Laci or Scott standing there with an armload of fresh tomatoes, carrots or other homegrown goodies. Sometimes the veggies were simply left on porches for the neighbors to find for themselves.

Laci also loved to cook, especially gourmet meals, and she doted on her role as hostess when she and Scott invited family, friends and neighbors to their home to celebrate holidays or other special occasions. She went all out to make the events memorable.

The couple also hosted a Christmas party in 2001 and, according to the *Modesto Bee*, Laci made a surprise dish she called "figs in a blanket," an offering the cook conjured up herself from figs wrapped in slices of bacon. The dish was typical of Laci — creative, imaginative and fun.

When they threw a party on New Year's Eve, Laci was prettied up in an ankle-length blue skirt with a long-sleeve white shirt that tied in the front. A chalkboard announced the menu for dinner: carrot soup, cheese-onion torte and chicken in red wine sauce. Laci had whipped up chocolate mousse with fresh oranges for dessert.

Always a gracious hostess, Laci made certain to have the cooking done by the time guests arrived, even though it would be a couple of hours before everyone was seated at the table to begin the meal. Her favorite dinners were formal, not casual. Guests at Laci's house didn't dine on chicken wings from the nearest sports bar, Chinese carry-out or pizza that tasted like cardboard. Everything was carefully planned, carried out and always first-class. No one left dinner hungry — but guests were expected to do their part by showing up dressed in their best for the occasion.

At other times, Laci enjoyed letting her hair down and hosting less formal events, including pool parties and backyard barbecues. Scott showed off his own cooking prowess at the cookouts, doing the honors as senior chef on the backyard barbecue he had built himself.

With the couple's efforts, the home at 523 Covena Avenue in Modesto became a warm and welcoming place, one where friends and family gathered to enjoy the good life.

Chapter 5

CONNER

Early in June 2002, just short of five years after Laci and Scott were married, she began telephoning family and friends with the joyful news — she was pregnant!

Laci was so thrilled and excited when she found out about the expected baby that she started calling around at 7 o'clock in the morning, waking up some of the recipients with her happy announcement.

Because she had one of her ovaries removed, it was more difficult for Laci to become pregnant. "She figured that maybe she will get pregnant and maybe she won't," said Beth Bashaw, a close family friend who lives on Laci's father's ranch north of Modesto. The expectant mom was "giddy" over the good news, Bashaw added.

"We feared she might not be able to have children, so when it happened, it was just like a miracle for us," Laci's delighted dad, Dennis Rocha, chimed in.

Since birth, Laci proved to be the perfect daughter, perfect friend and perfect wife, according to those who knew her best — and they were convinced she had the desire and ability to be a perfect mother to her child. She already treasured her nephew, Antonio Rocha, who was born in 1999, and looked forward to spoiling her own child.

After Laci had made her calls to friends and family, she went out and cleared store shelves of every parenting book she could find. She was barely three months along and hardly showing at all when she began proudly sporting maternity clothes. Just to make sure that everything proceeded properly, she quit her job as a substitute teacher to devote herself full time to homemaking, gardening and approaching motherhood.

Laci also joined a class for expectant mothers at the Village Yoga Center in

McHenry Village designed to teach exercise and relaxation techniques. Laci missed a few early sessions because she was having dizzy spells, but it wasn't very long before she was a regular. She drew understanding chuckles from the four other women in the class when she consistently arrived 10 minutes late and as soon as she got in the door, headed straight for the bathroom.

Soon enough, an ultrasound confirmed that Laci was carrying a boy and she announced to everybody she knew that she had already picked out his name — Conner.

Laci was determined to do everything right, according to her yoga partner, Elizabeth Te Velde. The baby "was the center of her whole world," the woman said. Te Velde was already the mother of two when she met Laci at the twice-a-week class. "She talked constantly about Conner, how she wanted everything to be just right for him when he was born," Te Velde said. "She didn't talk much about her husband, Scott, and I never saw him at yoga with her."

When Laci learned the baby was a boy, she instructed Scott to paint the nursery with a bright blue nautical motif. Conner's father was a sport fisherman and she wanted pictures of ships and fish on the walls. The room was furnished with a rocking chair, crib and a changing table that the father-to-be built himself. Neighbors smiled approvingly as Scott hauled the crib and a mattress into the house shortly before Thanksgiving. La Loma was a nice, friendly neighborhood, and the idea of a new baby on the way made it even nicer.

"I know he put a lot of hours into making that baby room just right," Guy Miligi, a friend of the Petersons, said of Scott. "He was real excited about having his first child. He talked about that all the time."

At the yoga class, Laci was busy firing questions at other women who had already given birth. Te Velde was about to have her third child and Laci grilled her about what she should do if the baby cried too much, if he didn't take his milk and what sort of toys she should buy for him.

"Laci had dreams and hopes for her little Conner," Te Velde recalled. "He was going to play Little League baseball, he'd go to a university and become a doctor, or a famous writer or be a success in business. But then she told me: 'I'm not really worried about what he grows up to be. I just want him to be happy.'"

Demonstrating that the expectant mom was still a daddy's girl, she confided to a friend, Melinda Freeman, that with a son on the way, her life was complete and she hoped Conner would grow up to become a dairy farmer just like her father. "I remember going to the milking sheds on those beautiful mornings. I will make sure my son has lots of exposure to animals," Laci told Freeman.

About a week before Christmas, Laci and Scott were with his parents in Carmel when they spent some time looking at cars. Jackie Peterson later recalled that her daughter-in-law wanted a vehicle that would be safer for her baby and was thinking of trading in her SUV.

As Laci prepared to welcome her son into the world with loving arms, doctors told her she could expect the baby boy to make his appearance early the next year, on or around Feb. 10, but ultimately, the exact date would be Conner's call.

Chapter 6

AMBER

As Laci's belly swelled, she was thrilled with the drastic change in her silhouette because it meant that Conner was growing and developing into the little person who would so dramatically transform and brighten the lives of his parents.

The expectant father was less enthusiastic. The further Laci's pregnancy progressed, the more distant her previously attentive husband became. He wasn't as romantic as he used to be and he began keeping late hours away from home and spending weekends on business trips. And he wasn't showing the same enthusiasm about becoming a dad as he had previously expressed to friends.

Scott explained to Laci, sometimes patiently and sometimes not, that he had to work harder now that a baby was on the way. Selling chemical fertilizer, after all, was demanding and difficult work.

Laci was disappointed at the development. She hadn't expected Scott's waning appetite for romance and had thought he would view her pregnancy as she did — a sort of baby-makes-three bonding experience.

When he wasn't on business trips, spending a late night with a client, or off fishing or golfing somewhere, Scott spent a lot of time getting his hair styled, trimmed or dyed at Salon Salon. One hairdresser later recalled that, "He thought he was quite the stud and was definitely always looking at the ladies."

One of the ladies Scott was taking the closest look at was a lithe blonde massage therapist and single mother he met while he was on a business trip to Fresno, less than a two-hour drive southeast along California State Highway 99 from the cozy home he and Laci had made for themselves in Modesto.

Amber Frey was a 27-year-old gray-eyed beauty who Scott met on a blind date at the

World Sports Café bar in Fresno on Nov. 20. The date was set up by another woman who worked with Scott but believed he was single.

Amber told Scott the evening they met that she didn't want anything to do with a man who was married or separated from his wife. The single mom with a 2-year-old daughter had been stung once before when she dated a married man.

The handsome salesman assured her that he was footloose and fancy free, with no wife lurking somewhere in his background. He had never been married. With that said, Amber was free to size up her personable, athletic-looking date — and she liked what she saw.

During their next few dates when he was in town, the new man in her life impressed her as charming and a good conversationalist who was understanding and attentive to her. He looked like a good catch and excellent husband material.

Amber's successful contractor dad, Ron Frey, was also happy his daughter had found a new and caring boyfriend. Ron and his mother baby-sat Amber's little girl while the young couple went on dates.

On Dec. 14, Amber decided to show Scott off at the $25-a-head Christmas bash at the World Sports Café in Fresno where they had first met. He bought the tickets and she spent days shopping for just the right outfit to please her man. Her sister, Ava, later confided that the party was "a big deal" to Amber and she talked of nothing else for a week.

Scott arranged to be in Fresno on the big night and Amber didn't disappoint him when he showed up at her door. She was lovely in a glamorous red strapless gown that showed off her slender figure and brought a gasp of admiration from her boyfriend. Scott was dressed to perfection in a dark suit with a flower in his buttonhole and he bowled over Amber's girlfriends with his suave appearance, courteous chatter and attentiveness to his date.

When Amber overheard Scott talking enthusiastically about her to someone else she asked, "What exactly is our relationship?"

"I want us to be exclusive," he replied, making it clear that he meant they shouldn't be dating anyone else. Then he planted a warm, affectionate kiss on her lips and told her, "You're my baby girl." Scott also said he planned to ask his boss for an OK to cut down on his travel so he could spend more time with her.

At a girlfriend's house after the party, someone was taking pictures and the happy couple posed with big smiles on their faces and their arms around each other for one shot in front of a gaily decorated Christmas tree topped with a silver star. Their hands were clasped lovingly together.

An excited Amber was convinced that she and the beguiling new man in her life had a real future together. She sent one of the photos of her and Scott together to her grandmother tucked into a Christmas card. She also confided to her father, Ron, that she might be moving to Modesto so she could be with the handsome hunk who was suddenly playing such an important role in her life.

"She was in love and very proud of him," Ron later recalled. "They had their picture taken ... and she handed me a copy and said happily, 'This is me and my boyfriend.' " They had another photograph taken together at a professional studio. "Just like any serious couple would," Frey added.

Scott knew how to strike the romantic chords in a woman's heart and instinctively understood just what to do to make Amber feel special. He noticed little things about women and capitalized on the information to spice up an affair with captivating surprises that were touchingly intimate.

One time, after learning what Amber's favorite apple was, he secretly brought one back to her apartment. Then he cooked up some caramel, covered the apple with it and served the sweet, chewy confection to her on a plate with all the pomp, flourishes and formality to which a princess would be treated. Scott followed up the romantic gesture by cleaning up the kitchen until it was spic and span. Amber told her sister how sweet she thought his performance was.

A little less than a week before Christmas, the first evidence of mold began to form, soiling the edges of the idyllic romance and triggering doubts in Amber's mind. Scott appeared at her apartment in tears. Amber was shocked and asked the big, bawling hunk what he was so upset about.

"I have to tell you something," he blubbered. "I lied to you when I told you I'd never been married before."

"What do you mean, you lied?" she asked.

"I lost my wife," he replied. He looked

miserable and tears were running down his cheeks. "I lost her the first week of December last year."

The shocked woman assumed that when Scott said he lost his wife, he meant she was dead and that he was a widower.

"What? You've been telling me how much our relationship meant to you — and now you admit you lied?" she demanded.

Scott claimed that his tears were not for his wife, but were for Amber because he felt so bad about lying to her. He dearly wanted to keep their relationship honest.

The confrontation ended in an uneasy standoff.

But then Scott set off more alarm bells in his girlfriend's mind when he explained that he wouldn't be able to celebrate Christmas with her because he was going to spend the holiday with his family in Maine before flying to Paris on a business trip. He didn't expect to return home until Jan. 25, but promised to keep in touch with daily phone calls.

Amber asked for his family's address in Maine so she could send him a present. He evasively told her to simply send the gift to a post office box he had in Modesto. On top of all that, Scott hadn't yet bought a Christmas gift for her, nor would he.

The unexpected developments disappointed Amber — the unnerving revelation about his "late wife" and his mysterious unavailability over Christmas and New Year's Eve. She wondered, what kind of person wouldn't do everything they could to be with their sweetheart over the holidays? She had a chum who was a private detective and she asked him to check out the charming, silver-tongued boyfriend whose behavior had become so suddenly peculiar.

Chapter 7

PREPARATIONS

Leading a double life as the husband of one woman and the boyfriend of another who lived 90 miles away while preparing for the birth of a baby was an exhausting, brain-bending business. Scott had maneuvered himself into a terrible mess and he was desperate to find a way out.

Along with all the other demons chasing him, Scott and Laci were coping with serious money problems even before learning there was a baby on the way. They had already declared bankruptcy once, then went right back to their reckless spending ways. It was estimated that they had run up new debts as high as $100,000 after giving up on The Shack.

Laci entertained friends often and lavishly, and the couple had a pool man and a part-time maid. Scott loved big boy toys, accumulating everything from golf clubs and fishing tackle to a 2002 Ford F-150 pickup truck and a 14-foot aluminum boat. Laci had her own expensive Range Rover. Scott even shelled out a whopping $25,000 just for a membership in Modesto's exclusive Del Rio Country Club.

Thanks mostly to their high-living lifestyle and backbreaking mortgage payments, their money was going out faster than it was coming in. A few weeks after Laci unexpectedly became pregnant, Scott took out a $250,000 life insurance policy on her, making himself the beneficiary and not the expected child. Laci took out a smaller policy on her husband at the same time.

According to some reports, he was chatting with a friend early in December about manure ponds that dot the Central California Valley dairy farmland like worked-out mineshafts in Pennsylvania or West Virginia when he made a comment that, in retrospect, was downright chilling.

"What a great place to hide a body," the fertilizer salesman is said to have observed.

Hundreds of the toxic ponds send up their noxious odors and poisonous gases from pastures surrounding Modesto. For every hundred cows, the average dairy farm will have a pond that is 100 feet wide at the top, 30 feet wide on the bottom and 15 feet deep. They are used to collect the waste product of cows. The ponds are maintained with chemical additives because there's a constant buildup of methane gas, which can be explosive. And the slime-filled bodies of water are so toxic, in fact, that a human body would disintegrate beyond recognition in a very short period of time.

Even with all the pressures building on him, Scott's busy schedule and complicated life wasn't all work and no play. He kept his word to Amber to telephone her while supposedly in Maine, but was curiously evasive in the conversations. Scott, of course, never left California and he was involved in some exceedingly strange activities.

The philandering husband was like a little boy whose eyes were bigger than his belly. He had heaped too much on his dinner plate and now he had to deal with it. It was only a matter of time, and not very much time at that, before his money troubles, lies and deceptions caught up with him. When that happened he would find himself facing tragic results.

The facade Scott had so carefully constructed while attempting to juggle the two women in his life was rapidly crumbling. Laci discovered her husband's seamy sexual dalliance with the long-legged beauty from Fresno and she hit the roof. About Dec. 21 or 22, she found photographs of Scott with Amber and they tangled in a blazing fight. Laci was already concerned and suspicious about the frequent business trips and the late hours he was keeping and the incriminating photographs put everything together for her. While she was carrying their baby, he was fooling around and spending money on another woman. Laci told her straying husband that the marriage was over and that it was going to cost him plenty. He was going to be paying alimony — and child support.

Laci didn't want to spoil the holidays for her family and decided to keep the marital troubles from them until after Christmas, sources later confided. She kept up a pretense of normalcy, even buying, wrapping and placing gifts for Scott under the Christmas tree as part of the painful charade. Scott reportedly didn't bother to buy or wrap any gifts for her.

He did, however, put in some time surfing the Web on his computer for information he used to construct five cement anchors, mixing up a batch of cement and pouring it into buckets to make the heavy concrete weights. Scott also ordered five new 55-gallon metal drums a few days before Christmas. But one of his most intriguing purchases was a set of ankle weights.

Late in December, Scott was back on the Internet looking up the time of high tide at the Berkeley Marina on San Francisco Bay. He learned that around Christmas, high tide would occur there shortly after midnight, in the pre-dawn hours.

Chapter 8

A FISHING TRIP

On the early evening of Dec. 23, investigators believe, Scott Peterson put a deadly plan that had been simmering in his mind into action. A careful reconstruction of events led Modesto and California law enforcement authorities to believe that sometime within a couple of hours or less after Laci last spoke with her mother on the telephone, she was murdered in the kitchen of the couple's home.

According to a chilling scenario, the helpless mother-to-be was punched in the stomach and beaten to death by her cheating husband after she got dressed for bed.

"Cops believe Laci may have been beaten to death with blows hard enough to make her throw up," said a police insider. "It brings up the nightmare that Laci, eight months pregnant, was punched in the stomach prior to her death."

The source also raised the possibility that Laci may have been bound, gagged, choked and tied to a red kitchen chair before she was killed.

"There are rub marks on the chair that could have been from a rope," the insider disclosed. "Laci definitely suffered before she died. Her final minutes were filled with pain and terror."

Scott had told Laci he was going to use his pickup to haul his 14-foot boat to the Berkeley marina and do some fishing the next morning, police believe. Laci never mentioned the fishing trip when she talked with her mother, "so it seems clear he brought it up after Laci hung up with her mom," said the insider.

Investigators suspect Scott might have been pushing Laci into a quarrel or else she may have accused him of lying, saying he was really planning to see Amber the next day instead of going fishing. "Police know violence erupted right then and there in the kitchen of the Peterson home," the insider declared.

How could anyone commit such a heinous act — brutally murdering his pregnant wife and unborn child? Police believe Scott's desire to remain free to carry on his affair with Amber and pursue other women led him to commit the crime.

Although Laci was overjoyed when she learned of her pregnancy, at the same time Scott didn't want to be a father. He told his secret lover, Amber, that if he married her he was probably going to have a vasectomy, according to a member of her family.

"Investigators think Scott planned to kill Laci and came up with an idea to make it look like she'd been abducted near their home while he was fishing 90 miles away," said the source. Scott didn't realize, however, that Laci's disappearance would make headlines around the world and he'd be forced to feed lie after lie to her family, the media and police.

According to the scenario based on evidence discovered during the investigation, police theorized that after committing the brutal murder, Scott loaded his wife's body into his Ford F-150 pickup truck under the cover of darkness late on Dec. 23. Then he drove to the Modesto warehouse he used for his fertilizer sales job.

"There he stuffed 5-foot-1-inch Laci into one of the 55-gallon drums he'd ordered, packed it with the cement anchors he'd made and covered the drum with its lid," the insider said. Cops found five circular impressions in the dust at Scott's warehouse, made from the upturned buckets he used to mold the anchors, but Scott could only account for two of the five anchors. That lead them to believe he used the remaining three in the disposal of his wife's body.

At last the heavy drum was loaded into the bed of the truck and after hooking up his boat kept at his warehouse, Scott made the approximate 90-minute drive to the Berkeley Marina on San Francisco Bay. He is believed to have exited Interstate 80 at Gilman Street. He passed the Radisson Hotel on the marina grounds, drove slowly along a single lane that took him through Cesar Chavez Park and ended at a parking lot by the rock-strewn slope that leads to the water of San Francisco Bay.

It's possible to drive a truck along a path by the shore, a walkway where benches are dedicated to lost loved ones. At that time of the morning, the marina would have been dark, totally deserted and hidden from view by a grassy hill. Seagulls weren't even stirring yet.

It was high tide when Scott lifted the barrel out of the truck under the cover of faint moonlight, momentarily steadied it on the edge of the ground and then gave it a shove. The barrel rolled down the rocky incline and plopped into the chilly water. It would have taken only a few minutes for the barrel to float out into the bay with the tide and slowly sink with its human cargo from the weight of the anchors and from water gradually filling it up. It finally came to rest quietly at the bottom of the bay among the crabs, the mollusks and oily silt.

"Scott then drove back home by the time the sun came up," said the insider.

No one except Scott knows for certain what was on his mind as he guided the pick-up truck through the darkness on the lonely drive back to Modesto. But with Laci dead and her body disposed of, it was time for Scott to put the third and final phase of the ugly scheme into motion and build on the flimsy alibi he had worked out. Sometime either before the drive to Berkeley or after returning home, Scott is believed to have mopped the kitchen floor and scrubbed up.

A few hours after daylight, according to the scenario, he climbed back into the light brown pickup truck and with the boat trailing securely behind, he drove to a food store and other places around town. It was important to his alibi that he be seen with the boat and remembered as a young man who was apparently on his way to do some fishing.

Longtime Modesto resident Connie Fleeman was buying cigarettes when she bumped into Scott in a food shop in Modesto at 10 a.m. that morning. He was drinking a can of Red Bull, an energy drink that's loaded with caffeine. It is often the choice of bodybuilders and students who need to keep awake and alert. Scott had put in a long, busy night and he still had a lot of important chores to do.

"I literally bumped him coming out of Crescent Food City on Coffee Road," Connie said. "He hit me with the door of his truck and we joked about it. I told him I'd been admiring his truck and boat because they were both so clean.

"In the truck was an overstuffed green tool box with a gray cloth covering something sticking out of the top. The boat the truck was towing was empty. There was no ice chest, no life vest, no fishing poles and no tackle box. He didn't appear to be a man going fishing." There was also no evidence of any fishing tackle in his truck.

Connie noticed one more curious thing. He was too neatly dressed, she said. "He wore a sparkling white polo shirt with a collar. He also had on neatly pressed blue cotton twill pants and a red-and-beige plaid jacket," she said. "Most guys wear old clothes when they go fishing — but he was immaculate."

The two went their separate ways, but shortly after it was publicly disclosed that Laci disappeared, Connie saw a police appeal for anyone who'd seen Scott's truck and boat on Dec. 24 to come forward, so she passed on her information to police.

"They also had his picture and I thought, 'That's the guy I saw at the store,' " added Connie.

Crescent Food City owner Fred Hanna confirmed Connie and Scott were in the store at the same time.

Scott wanted to be seen, according to a police insider. "It helped him create the illusion that he was headed off to go fishing and was many miles away from his home when Laci vanished."

Once back in Berkeley, Scott reinforced that alibi by simply putting $5 into the yellow parking fee machine at the marina boat launch. The parking ticket had a time and date stamped on it.

Later in the day, he drove back to 523 Covena Avenue, parked the truck and boat outside just as if he was returning after a day-long fishing expedition to San Francisco Bay and walked into the house. A neighbor, Amie Krigbaum, noticed the truck outside the house when she returned to her home about 5:15 p.m., after a trip to the store. Almost exactly 15 minutes later, Scott ran across the street, pounded on her door and asked Amie and her roommate, Terra Venable, if they had seen his wife.

He was "teary-eyed and seemed to be in a panic mode," Amie later confided. He said he'd been trying to call Laci on his cell phone all day, but couldn't reach her. Then when he got home, she wasn't there. The roommates hadn't seen anything of Laci, and Scott left, running up and down the street, calling for his wife.

There was something about the apparently

frantic husband that struck Amie as curious. "The strange thing was that, when he came rushing over, he was clean and nicely dressed in a blue long-sleeved dress shirt and khaki dress pants," she recalled. "He didn't look like a guy who'd just been fishing."

There was something else that was peculiar. When Amie left for the store at about 4:45 p.m., Scott's truck wasn't in the driveway, but it was parked there in its usual place when she returned home at about 5:15. "But he didn't come running over till 5:30. I don't know how long he'd been home, but it was at least 15 minutes and could have been more than half an hour."

Scott telephoned family members and friends of his wife, telling them she was missing and asking if they knew where she was. Sharon Rocha later remembered that she and her husband were expecting her daughter and son-in-law for dinner when Scott telephoned and asked if Laci was there. The suddenly alarmed woman told him "no."

"He said, 'Well the car is here and the dog was in the backyard with his leash on and Laci's missing,'" she recalled.

When Scott called Laci's half-sister, Amy,

he didn't bother saying hello or identifying himself. He simply blurted out the question, "Is your sister with you?" He sounded panicky and emotional. Scott dialed up several of her girlhood chums and asked the same question. Of course they hadn't heard from or seen Laci, but several of them hurried to the house where she had entertained them so lavishly so many times and asked what they could do to help.

It was a few minutes before 6 p.m. when Scott phoned the Grantskis with the frightening news. Ron Grantski immediately notified police that his stepdaughter was missing from her home — and she was in the late stages of pregnancy. He made the call at just about the time the family had expected to be sitting down to a sumptuous dinner that was already prepared and waiting for the young couple to arrive at the Grantski home so they could all celebrate the holiday together.

Scott told his neighbor, Amie, that he called police. But he never did file a police report notifying them about his missing wife. He didn't even get around to notifying his own parents about his wife's distressing absence until the next day — Christmas morning.

According to his account, later related to police, he left home at about 9:30 Tuesday morning, Dec. 24, and headed for the Berkeley Marina to spend the day fishing for sturgeon in San Francisco Bay. Laci was planning to walk her dog, McKenzie, in the park and then do some Christmas shopping. The house was only about 100 yards from a footpath leading into the park and it was a popular spot for dog-walkers as well as joggers, cyclists and inline skaters.

Scott said that he tried dialing his wife from his cell phone during the drive back from the Bay, but she didn't respond. When he arrived home late in the afternoon, there was no sign of her. She hadn't left a note for him and her purse, keys and cell phone were where she always left them. Her SUV was parked in its usual space in the driveway.

McKenzie was penned up in the backyard. A neighbor later revealed that he spotted the 8-year-old golden retriever mix wandering the streets about 10:30 that morning, trailing a muddy leash attached to his collar, and took him home.

By dusk, everyone in the neighborhood knew that the young homemaker and expectant mother was missing and scores of concerned men and women joined her husband in a search of La Loma Park.

Lieutenant Bruce Able and about a half-dozen other officers from the Modesto Police Department also headed for the park, even though it was already shrouded in darkness. The local Stanislaus County Sheriff's Department pitched in with a helicopter and two pilots to fly a search pattern along Dry Creek. The helicopter was equipped with a huge searchlight that was beamed along the rugged creek and shoreline, and a heat-sensing device was also activated.

Other officers from the city police department began filtering through the neighborhood, stopping concerned neighbors on the street and knocking on doors in hopes of gathering information that would be helpful in locating the missing woman. They talked with some people who said they saw Laci walking her dog in the park about 10 a.m. They also interviewed the neighbor who found McKenzie wandering the streets and returned him to the Peterson's backyard.

Police worked through most of the night and by daybreak they were back with reinforcements that swelled the search team to about 30 officers, along with a squad of firefighters. By early afternoon Christmas Day, a phalanx of officers were stretched out side-by-side making a meticulous sweep of the park from the El Vista bridge downstream to Beard Brook Park near Yosemite Boulevard.

Six firefighters climbed into an inflatable raft equipped with water-rescue gear and floated down the rocky creek, staring apprehensively into the cold water and intently peering into the bushes lining the shoreline. Three Modesto police officers mounted on horses and two others on bicycles were assigned to the growing operation. Five K-9 units were summoned to help. Police also checked out areas of the park that were known encampments for the homeless. But the squatters were spooked by all the fuss and the heavy police presence. Most of them had already cleared out.

Civilian volunteers joined police who fanned out through the neighborhood, venturing into yards, checking alleys and poking through discarded trash — anything that might be big enough to conceal a body. Jeff Tomlinson of nearby Hughson was among the volunteers. His wife, Rene — one of Laci's closest friends — was already planning a baby shower in a couple of weeks for her old high school chum. The last time

Rene talked with her friend was a few days earlier, when Laci told her she was going out to buy fabric for the nursery.

Other friends stationed themselves along entrances to the park, staring hopefully into the darkness as if they were hoping she would come bouncing along the path, beaming with her trademark smile and asking what all the fuss was about.

The first fliers seeking information about the missing woman were also prepared and distributed on Christmas Day. They were handed out in the neighborhood and at shopping centers, and others were tacked to telephone poles or taped to the windows of storefronts by her friends. Many Christmas dinners that day went unprepared or uneaten. It was a gloomy holiday for friends and neighbors of the missing woman.

When family members rushed to the house after Scott notified them that Laci was missing, they found it was gaily decorated for the holidays with presents under the Christmas tree. But they were shocked when they realized that Laci left presents for Scott, but he hadn't left anything for her, an insider revealed.

Family members, friends and others who

had never before heard of Laci Peterson streamed in from all over California to help with the search and to comfort the people who loved her most. The family set up their headquarters for the volunteer effort at Scott and Laci's house. The Modesto Police Department established its own on-scene command post at East La Loma Park.

It seemed that no one knew if Laci was dead or alive. She may not have even been in the park, which was the initial focus of the rapidly broadening search. There was a chance that she may have been kidnapped, as her husband said he feared, and spirited away.

But there was another possibility that police had already begun to consider — that Scott Peterson might know far more than he was revealing.

Chapter 9

SUSPICIONS

Among all known murders of women across the country in 2000, the most recent yearly statistics available from the U. S. Department of Justice, more than 33 percent were killed by a spouse or lover. Almost daily, somewhere in the United States, a wife is strangled, shot, beaten to death or killed in some other way by a husband or significant other. Many of the slayings are the culmination of long-term abuse that began during courtship and then continued for months or years before the final lethal confrontation. Others can be less predictable — cool, deliberate acts that are carefully plotted in advance.

Conjugal slayings, the murder of one's life partner, is the worst possible betrayal because the killer is the individual the victim should be most able to trust. Yet it is a shockingly common type of homicide. It's so common, in fact, that when either a married man or woman becomes a homicide victim, the first person that police turn to as a potential suspect is often the spouse.

No one knew yet if Laci was the victim of a homicide, but she was missing under exceedingly ominous circumstances that led the people who loved her, as well as investigators, to suspect the worst. And one of the first people that Modesto homicide detectives began taking a close look at as the potential key to solving the mystery was her husband, Scott. But they had more than dry statistics to make them suspicious of the husband and the glib story he was telling.

While they were questioning neighbors, investigators learned that the first thing Laci did every morning after getting out of bed was to pull open the window shades. Curiously, the shades were never opened on Dec. 24, although according to her husband's story, she was home and awake to see him off when he left on his fishing trip. Leaving the drapes closed would have been more than simply out of character for her; it was something she absolutely would not have done.

A neighbor also reported noticing Scott lugging something heavy and wrapped in a blue tarpaulin from the house shortly before 9:30 a.m. Dec. 24 and dumping it into his truck. Scott later said the tarp contained large backyard umbrellas he was taking to his warehouse for storage. But investigators suspected he may have been removing evidence from the scene of the crime.

At 7:45 a.m. Dec. 26, police showed up at the house with a search warrant. They found a wet mop in the kitchen. That piqued the curiosity of detectives because the maid told them she had mopped the floor last on Dec. 23, then wrung out the mop and left it to dry. Another witness told police that Scott also vacuumed the floor late on that evening.

Could he have been trying to get rid of bloodstains and other telltale evidence, authorities wondered?

Police believed the answer could lie in tests

conducted at a state forensics laboratory. Investigators sent specks of blood mixed with traces of vomit that were found in the kitchen, on the mop and in Scott's pickup truck to the Central Valley Regional Laboratory in nearby Ripon for serology tests. Clothing found in the laundry room was also shipped off for forensics tests at Ripon — another small farming community about a 10-minute drive from the dairy farm where Laci spent her early childhood.

Police were exploring whether Scott possibly used the mop to clean the kitchen after his wife was killed. Other evidence, including the witness accounts, indicated that after returning to the house on Christmas Eve, Scott was home at least 15 minutes, probably longer — and took time to shower and change clothes before showing up apparently distraught and knocking on the neighbor's door to ask about his wife. He also put the clothes he took off into the washer and turned it on before looking for help to locate his wife, a source disclosed.

When Scott talked with police, he told them the water in San Francisco Bay was rough and choppy while he was fishing and his clothes were soaked with seawater. But taking time to clean up and drop the soggy clothes in the wash before looking for his ominously missing wife smelled about as fishy to the suspicious investigators as a dead sturgeon floating belly up in the bay. Any normal husband returning home from a daylong trip to find his pregnant wife missing with no note or other explanation, but with her purse, keys and cell phone where she always left them, would have been frantic, they reasoned. Laci would have probably taken the belongings with her if she intentionally left the house.

Detectives and forensics technicians hauled off clothing, two personal computers and other undisclosed items of potential evidence. They also impounded Scott's pickup truck and his boat, which he said he used during the fishing trip.

On Thursday, bloodhounds were brought in by expert trackers in an attempt to pick up Laci's trail. One of the floppy-eared, big-nosed hounds was allowed to sniff an article of Laci's clothing, then released at 5 p.m. in front of the house. Afternoon is one of the best times for tracking dogs to work because scent is easier to pick up then. But the dog didn't head for the dirt path leading into the park as some expected it to do. It repeatedly led its handler to a spot in the Peterson's driveway.

With its nose close to the ground, another dog headed around the corner, then lumbered south to Yosemite Boulevard in the opposite direction from the park. It was dark by the time the hound began sniffing around a Dumpster and police officers climbed inside to look around with flashlights. A police department public relations specialist who dealt with the press wouldn't reveal if they found anything.

A flurry of excitement was set off the same day the house was searched when a neighbor returned home from a trip and discovered his back door had been kicked open and a safe carried away with contents that included $50,000 worth of jewelry and a couple of handguns. He lived just across the street from the Petersons. Another neighbor reported observing three suspicious men and a couple of vehicles outside the house around 11:30 on the morning Laci was said to have vanished, according to the *Modesto Bee*.

At first glance, the development sounded like police had a hot lead that might take them straight to the kidnappers who snatched Laci. It seemed totally logical to believe that Laci could have been in the wrong place at the wrong time and that the burglars panicked and carried her away when they realized she saw them breaking into the house and could be a potential eyewitness against them. When detectives learned that the breakin most likely occurred later than previously believed, after Laci disappeared, the theory was abandoned.

Scott had pointed to Christmas Eve as the day his wife dropped from sight, so throughout the early days of the investigation, stories in the print and electronic media consistently reported that Laci disappeared Dec. 24. But police were coming to a different conclusion about the time of her disappearance. They were intent, however, on protecting the investigation and didn't immediately share information pointing to Dec. 23 as the critical date with others outside law enforcement circles involved in the probe.

The Stanislaus County Sheriff's Department and the FBI had joined in the investigation and other law enforcement agencies, including state police, were also already playing various roles in the probe or soon would be. The FBI reportedly moved into the case because of the possibility of kidnapping, which is a federal crime.

Modesto police, still answering questions about the burglary, were cautious regarding tying the theft of the safe to the missing woman. They told reporters they hadn't immediately turned up anything concrete to suggest that the two troubling events in the La Loma neighborhood were linked.

Laci's 30-year-old brother, Brent, was less reticent about linking the burglary and his sister's disappearance. Recalling that one of the police bloodhounds lost his sister's scent a short distance from the house, he told reporters: "That leads me to believe that the robbers probably grabbed Laci right on the street."

Meanwhile, police were increasing their scrutiny on the man they believed might be responsible for Laci's disappearance and murder. Officially, the case was still being carried as a missing persons investigation, but detectives were working it as if it was a homicide. They were collecting an increasingly wide array of evidence and poking gaping holes in Scott's account of the last day he saw his wife and the mysterious fishing trip.

Modesto Police Chief Roy Wasden would

eventually sum things up when he said Scott was a suspect from the start of the case and described him as a "dumb criminal."

Authorities now were convinced Laci and her unborn child had been murdered and the evidence against Scott mounted. Some of the additional clues and peculiar behavior by the chief suspect included:

● Tests on Scott's fishing boat disclosed that it hadn't been in saltwater recently, apparently backing up the observations of Connie Fleeman when she encountered Scott at Crescent Food City. There were no traces of saltwater on the boat or on its engine — providing a strong indication that his story of fishing in San Francisco Bay was a flat-out lie.

● Scott was an experienced fisherman who would have known that midday wasn't the best time to be on the water if he was really serious about catching anything. Most fishermen like to be out on the water early in the morning when the fish are biting. "And that little boat is better for lake fishing than the rough waters of San Francisco Bay," a police insider revealed. "Experienced fishermen say they wouldn't go out on the bay in it."

● When an investigator questioned Scott as to what kind of bait he used on his supposed fishing trip, the suspect replied, "I don't remember." According to an insider, one of the detectives later said, "I can remember the bait I used on a fishing trip with my dad when I was 13 years old. And this guy couldn't remember what he'd used to try to hook sturgeon 48 hours ago?"

● Detectives interviewed workers at the marina and none of them could recall seeing Scott there on Dec. 24. "All he probably did was drive around and he finally returned home in the late afternoon to start calling around to say his wife was missing," said an investigative source.

● When police asked Scott about a couple of empty cement sacks found in the yard of his home, he explained that workmen for his pool contractor left them there. But when detectives interviewed the contractor, he denied that his employees left the sacks.

● The behavior of the bloodhound that scented Laci's clothing and then repeatedly led its handler to the Peterson's driveway indicated that Laci didn't leave her home on foot. She was driven away in a vehicle. And the second bloodhound's interest in the Dumpster on Yosemite Boulevard, blocks from Laci's house, indicated that Scott possibly dumped evidence of the crime there, but it had been emptied so they couldn't recover any clues.

● On Christmas Day, only a few hours after reporting his wife was missing, Scott asked a real estate agent about the possibility of selling his house. "The house hadn't even been searched by police yet," an insider revealed. "But Scott asked a real estate agent in his neighborhood — a woman who was helping to search for Laci — about ways he could sell his home."

● Shockingly, authorities learned Scott had sold some of Laci's jewelry and other treasured belongings — while the massive search for his missing wife was still in progress! "When the police went into Scott and Laci's house for the second time with a search warrant, they were looking as much for what WASN'T there as for what evidence they could find," an insider confided. "Watches, earrings and trinkets that Laci treasured were nowhere to be found. And police later established that Scott sold them."

Even as Scott continued to stick by his shaky alibi, authorities knew he was backing himself right into a five-by-nine cell in San Quentin's death row.

Chapter 10

THE SEARCH FOR LACI

Residents of Modesto were understandably shocked and appalled when they learned that one of their neighbors, a pregnant woman only a few weeks from giving birth, was missing and feared dead. But it wasn't the first time the community attracted the attention of the world for the worst kind of reason. Modesto had barely recovered from the fallout over a pair of earlier crimes that bathed the normally tranquil valley in a firestorm of unwanted publicity and notoriety.

A promising young life was snuffed out and the dazzling political career of the charismatic local congressman was ruined before the search for Washington, D.C., intern Chandra Levy ended with the discovery of her remains in the heavily wooded area of Rock Creek Park near her apartment early in 2002. The 24-year-old woman vanished on April 30, 2001, leading to an investigation that shined the spotlight on married Congressman Gary Condit as her clandestine lover.

Chandra was missing nearly 13 months before a man and his dog searching for turtles discovered human bones, a Walkman and jogging clothes on May 22. The cause of death is still unknown and no one has been charged in the suspected slaying, which occurred in an area where other young female joggers listening to music through earphones as they ran had been attacked by an assailant. Condit, a six-term Democratic congressman representing the Modesto area before becoming entangled in the sexually charged political scandal, was defeated in his bid for re-election.

Then there had been the four women

slaughtered in 1999 by a motel handyman who hated females. The victims weren't from Modesto, but their murders occurred near enough to the Joaquin Valley agriculture center that the city became the hub of the investigation and the away-from-home headquarters for most of the press attracted by the ghoulish crimes.

Cary Stayner readily confessed to slaying three sightseers near Yosemite National Park in February, then murdering and decapitating Yosemite naturalist Joie Armstrong after a chance meeting with the 26-year-old woman in July. The first victims were 42-year-old Carole Sund, her 16-year-old daughter, Juli, and 16-year-old Silvina Pelosso, a family friend who was an exchange student from Argentina.

After his arrest at a Sacramento nudist colony, Stayner explained that he was acting out sexual fantasies. Ironically, he claimed that none of his victims was sexually abused, but he dreamed for 30 years about killing females. Because Armstrong was killed in a national park, the homicidal handyman was sentenced to life in federal prison. The other three women were slain outside the park, and for that Stayner was sentenced to execution at the California State Prison at San Quentin.

Mrs. Sund's sorrowful parents, Francis and Carole Carrington, responded to the tragedy that had blighted their lives by establishing a foundation to help families offer rewards for information that might be helpful to law enforcement authorities in locating missing loved ones. They named it the Carole Sund/Carrington Memorial Reward Foundation — and it was based in Modesto. One of the cases they became involved in was the search for Chandra Levy.

Now Modesto was in the spotlight again. People were coping with new fears that a young woman — one of their own — had died a gruesome death at the hands of a heartless killer.

The people of Modesto and neighboring communities were dispirited and heartsick, but they were determined to do everything they could to help solve the mystery. Hundreds of volunteers joined with police to search for the missing woman.

Laci's family pitched in to start a reward fund. With an additional $25,000 contribution from the Carole Sund/Carrington Memorial Reward Foundation and an anonymous donor, the fund quickly swelled to $500,000. Thousands of flyers were cranked out that read:

MISSING
$500,000 REWARD
For Information Leading To A Safe Return
Laci (Rocha) Peterson
Age 27 Height 5'1"
Eyes: Brown Hair: Brown
8 Months Pregnant
Call MODESTO P. D. at 209-342-6166
or visit lacipeterson.com
Laci was last seen 12/24/02 at 9:30 a. m.
She was believed to be heading toward
Dry Creek in Modesto, CA to walk her
golden retriever. She was wearing a
white long sleeve shirt and black pants.
Laci also has a sunflower tattoo on her
left ankle.

The photos on the posters included a close-up of Laci's face flashing her familiar dimpled smile and another that showed her pregnant and sitting in an armchair while wearing a black pantsuit.

Before the end of the year, Laci's family moved their headquarters from the house to the California Room of the Red Lion Hotel. The three-story hotel with a swimming pool, bar, restaurant and conference rooms in downtown Modesto was also the civilian headquarters for the Sund/Pelosso/Armstrong search and for the hometown effort to find Chandra Levy. Local residents from around the city helped fund the command center and as many as 200 volunteers a day streamed in to ask what they could do. Eventually more than 2,000 people were filling out forms, answering telephones, downloading messages on the Laci Peterson Web site and distributing flyers, posters, ribbons and buttons.

Maps were mounted on the wall with yellow highlights, showing areas already searched by police and volunteers. Even with a war on and American soldiers overseas fighting in Operation Iraqi Freedom, thousands of messages from people praying for Laci and expressing their sympathy to her family streamed in. By the time Laci was missing for two weeks, Modesto police had logged more than 1,600 calls on their tip line and were checking out scores of promising leads.

One of the people offering help was Donna

Raley, a nurse, according to the *Modesto Bee*. She was the stepmother of Dena Raley, who was 36 years old when she dropped from sight in October 1999. The tiny, green-eyed woman who never topped 100 pounds in her life was in an abusive relationship when she vanished and, despite a spirited investigation by police, hasn't been seen since.

Donna showed up unannounced on the Grantski/Rocha doorstep a few days after Laci disappeared and told Sharon that she was a mother like her and her daughter was also missing. Donna said she was there to help and told Sharon about Wings of Protection — a support group for families of missing men, women and children which she and Chandra Levy's mother, Susan, formed.

Operated out of the Raley home in a gated Modesto community, Wings of Protection offers regular meetings for members to provide emotional support and grief counseling, operates a Web site, provides speakers for service clubs, helps people assemble DNA kits and does whatever else is necessary to help people deal with the fear and uncertainty generated by a missing loved one.

At the Grantski/Rocha home, the two mothers talked and cried together. Donna

Raley was one of thousands of people in Modesto and all around America who were touched by the agonizing plight of Laci's family and sincerely wanted to help.

Meanwhile, the hunt for Laci expanded to include a vast stretch of wetlands 10 miles west of Modesto and a state recreational area surrounding Tulloch Lake, about a 45-minute drive west of the city in the Sierra Nevada foothills. Divers from the Stanislaus and Calaveras County Sheriff's Departments combed the bottom of the scenic lake for three days while other searchers tramped through brush and trees along the shoreline without turning up any trace of the missing woman.

Divers also combed the San Luis Reservoir west of Los Banos. The San Luis is one of the largest off-stream reservoirs in the country, has 65 miles of shoreline and covers 13,800 acres. In parts of the reservoir, the waters are 300 feet deep. Sonar was used to scan the reservoir and several other freshwater lakes.

Another team of law enforcement officers accompanied by scuba divers, six dogs and six boats headed for the Berkeley Marina on San Francisco Bay. The dogs were specially trained to smell cadavers in the water and they criss-crossed the surface of the bay on the boats or scouted along the shoreline from the marina to Brooks Island, where Scott said he was trying to hook sturgeon when his wife disappeared. The daylong effort ended without turning up any trace of Laci, but a blue tarpaulin was recovered and retained as possible evidence.

Back in Modesto, civilian city employees carried out another sweep of La Loma Park and opened up and checked every manhole that was anywhere near the wooded area or the Peterson home, according to the *Modesto Bee*.

Drawing on resources from the command center, Laci's family organized three searches of their own on successive Saturdays, when most volunteers would be off work and have free time to help beat the bushes for the missing woman. Police assisted the family in the selection of search sites.

More than 350 people turned out the first Saturday, Feb. 8, to comb through pastures and wetlands in western Stanislaus and southern San Joaquin county. About 130 joined in to check out the area around the Don Pedro Reservoir in Tuolumne county the following Saturday. The third and final sweep was concentrated around the new Melones Reservoir and drew about 100 volunteers, with six teams of horses and 10 boats to search the dark waters. Throughout all the searches, there was no trace of Laci.

The massive effort and the special empathy generated by the idea of a pregnant woman in peril caught the imagination of the press and Laci's disappearance quickly became a major press event. Print and electronic media from around the country and world streamed into Modesto, snapping up hotel rooms at the Red Lion, the DoubleTree Hotel and filling up other hotels and motels in and around the city. Every day news crews converged on the volunteer center and the Modesto Police Department at the corner of 10th and G streets, looking for updates on the mystery.

Scott developed a daily routine, arriving at the command center about 8 a.m., checking the number of hits on the Web site — lacipeterson.com — and scanning through some of the e-mail. Occasionally he snacked on food donated by local restaurants for the volunteers. Before leaving, he always asked the volunteers to pray for his wife, then snatched up a fistful of fliers and waved goodbye. He always said the same thing: He was going to post the fliers around town.

"We found out later that what he was really doing was playing golf," one neighbor later revealed. "I was so disgusted I quit as a volunteer."

Scott also exhibited other inappropriate behavior that went unnoticed by volunteers at the command center, but was witnessed by a Red Lion employee. Hadrian Lesser, the hotel's room services manager, revealed to reporters that while the search was going on for Laci, Scott and his boss were in the hotel's bar on three consecutive nights "laughing and having a good time."

Scott did hardly any talking with the media and only a few days after Laci was reported missing, he stormed out of a press conference after reporters began asking police about the fishing trip to San Francisco Bay. He avoided press conferences after that, but he did issue a public statement that he wrote out with a black marker pen and hung at the volunteer center. It read:

"As I see every person come through this door, or out searching, I tell Laci about them, looking for her. Early this morning, I felt she could hear me. She thanks you. Laci's husband."

It was a touching message — if sincere.

Although some volunteers choked up at times or allowed their eyes to mist over with tears, Scott seemed to have excellent control of his emotions. His employers were aware of the tragedy that had intruded into his life and were supportive, giving him the time off to do whatever had to be done.

The missing woman's family also loyally stood by their son-in-law, assuring him of their faith in him and of their mutual desire to see the mystery solved. It was an agonizing ordeal for the Grantskis and the Rochas and, unlike Scott, their emotions were rubbed raw and obvious. One time while Amy was on the local news, she broke down, bursting out crying and couldn't even finish her sentence.

As time passed, some of Scott's behavior while friends and strangers were searching for his wife was about as inappropriate as it could be and added fuel to the growing suspicions that he wasn't the distraught, heartsick husband that he claimed to be.

At a candlelight vigil for Laci on New Year's Eve that attracted more than 1,000 people to East La Loma Park, Scott didn't sit and talk quietly with members of her family as he was expected to do. Instead, he roamed through the crowd, smiling and laughing with pals much of the time, reported the *Modesto Bee*.

At times, Scott seemed to have two faces. In conversations with friends and in rare statements picked up by the press, he appeared a worried husband and father-to-be who desperately wanted to find his missing wife. The other face he presented to police was that of a curiously reluctant husband who was less than cooperative with their efforts to solve the mystery of what happened to Laci.

When detectives asked Scott to take a polygraph test, he initially agreed, then backed out. He explained that his parents had advised him against it. His reaction to the proposal was a troubling development and extremely curious if he really had nothing to hide and was anxious to eliminate himself as a suspect in his wife's disappearance.

A couple of weeks after Scott's queer behavior during the candlelight vigil in the park, the press revealed that he had hired one of Modesto's most noted criminal defense attorneys — Kirk McAllister. An investigator employed by the lawyer interviewed La Loma-area residents about a strange van seen in the neighborhood about the time Laci was reported missing. Police detectives said they believed the van was being used by a landscaping crew.

While Scott was dodging a lie detector test and his lawyer had a detective chasing a mystery van, Laci's loved ones were organizing another candlelight vigil.

Early Friday evening, Jan. 31, candles were lit, porch lights flipped on and prayers said all over Modesto for the lost mother and her unborn son. The home of Laci's mother and stepfather was the center for the candlelight vigil, and family members, friends, neighbors and other concerned people joined them in the front yard for the somber observance. In the Grantski yard at exactly 7 p.m., with the same dull candlelight bathing the proceedings, family friend Rita Keller began the observance with a silent prayer.

"We pray that all the light here tonight will pierce the darkness and help us to find Laci," she said. The words were so soft and so bruised by her tears that it was difficult for many in the silent crowd to hear — but the speaker's sincerity and pain was clear and many people began to weep.

Laci's family posted a message on their

Web site inviting people around the world to share in the vigil. "Light a candle, say a prayer or think a positive thought for her return," they urged. "No particular faith is endorsed. Some will light candles to St. Jude, Holy Mary. Others will just light a plain candle, leave a porch light on or will stop for a moment of silence to send their positive prayer into the world."

On Feb. 10, the day Laci's son was due, some of her friends led by her half-sister, Amy, gathered at La Loma Park just after sunset for yet another candlelight vigil. They read poetry and prayed.

Scott failed to attend these vigils and was also nowhere to be seen three days later, when his family announced at a press conference in San Diego that they were contacting hospitals and clinics around the country to determine if Laci may have been admitted and given birth.

Earlier the same day, Laci's fellow students at the Village Yoga Center released a bouquet of blue and yellow balloons and hung a plaque on the wall to show their concern and empathy for their missing prenatal classmate. The touching tribute read: "February 10, 2003. This is lovingly dedicated to Laci Denise Peterson and son Conner. Always in our hearts, forever in our prayers." The women prayed and shared anecdotes about their friend who was due to graduate that day by giving birth to her son. They also shed a lot of tears.

Laci was on just about everybody's mind. People speculated about Laci on the job, while they were shopping and wherever they gathered, night or day. Children at many area schools wore blue and yellow ribbons to show their empathy for the missing substitute teacher.

Every time a woman in the late terms of pregnancy showed up anywhere in Modesto — and in many other California communities — people did a double take.

Everyone was hoping to spot Laci alive.

As media coverage of the baffling case mushroomed, sightings of the missing woman were reported all over California and in other West Coast and neighboring states.

Police in Tempe, Arizona, home of Arizona State University, Scott's alma mater, and the Sun Devils, checked out an anonymous report that Laci was spotted standing near a parked car. An officer interviewed people in the area for an hour, but was unable to turn up any evidence confirming the sighting.

In Longview, Washington, just across the Columbia River from the Oregon state line, a grocery store cashier reported in late January that she saw Laci the previous month — when the pregnant woman begged her to call police. The 45-year-old cashier said the woman and a much older man with a ruddy complexion were in her checkout lane at The Market Place when he left to get something he forgot, giving his companion an opportunity to blurt out: "This is serious. I was kidnapped. Call the authorities when I leave." She also reportedly warned that her rough-looking companion had a gun.

The clerk explained that she planned to notify police but she couldn't find a phone book to obtain the number. Then she became distracted and forgot about the encounter until she saw a television report on the search for Laci and realized that was the woman who had pleaded for help.

The Longview Police Department dutifully checked out the unlikely story. Investigators meticulously reviewed the cashier's recollections with her and looked at more than 45 hours of video surveillance tape before concluding that there was no evidence in the footage indicating that Laci was ever in the store.

"Our hearts go out to the family of Laci Peterson," Police Chief Bob Burgreen told reporters at a press conference after dismissing the sighting as being wide of the mark. "We had hoped that this could possibly be a breakthrough lead but we now believe that is not the case."

The fanciful yarn had sounded suspiciously cockeyed to Laci's family from the start. Acting spokeswoman Kim Petersen said they never took the story seriously. "It didn't make sense from the beginning," she told reporters. "I mean, how many times does a pregnant woman walk into a store and say she's being kidnapped. How could you forget something like that?" Kim, who was no relation to Scott, was executive director of the Carole Sund-Carrington Memorial Reward Foundation that coordinated the volunteer efforts.

On another front, the blood test results were back from the laboratory and police obtained new warrants for Scott and Laci's house and other property. As TV cameras rolled, on Tuesday, Feb. 18 — only eight days after little Conner's expected delivery date — investigators returned to the house to begin a search that was even more extensive than the first. A big sign stood in the front yard announcing a reward for information leading to Laci's safe return. Police also combed through Scot's rented warehouse on Emerald Avenue.

It was about 8 a.m. when detectives saw Scott driving down Covena Avenue in his 2000 white Dodge Ram and stopped him. After the first search warrants were served back on Dec. 26, police had returned Laci's beloved Range Rover but kept Scott's 2002 light brown Ford F-150 pickup. He had then traded in the SUV to buy the Dodge. Now police seized that pickup truck. Without any transportation, Scott hung around, talking with detectives in his driveway and scribbling notes on a legal pad.

A few minutes after noon, Laci's half-sister, Amy, was escorted through the yellow crime scene tape and inside the house by officers to help with the search. She remained about two hours before leaving without talking to reporters, but appeared distressed.

So many motorists attracted by radio and TV reports were driving up and down the street in front of the house that police sealed

off the 500 block of Covena. So the rubber-
neckers parked their cars and walked to the
house to watch the show. A UPS delivery
man was turned away when he tried to
deliver a package for Laci from a wine-of-
the-month club.

By this point, law enforcement agencies
participating in the search included the
Modesto Police Department, the California
State Department of Justice, the Sacramento
Valley Hi-Tech Crimes Task Force and at
least one investigator with the Stanislaus
County District Attorney's Office. Detectives,
evidence technicians and police photogra-
phers rifled through the house like a cyclone.
They probed into walls, peered into piping
from sinks and toilets and went over everything with a fine-tooth comb.

Outside, other officers busied themselves
making measurements of the house, the
driveway, the converted garage and other
areas. Everything was carefully recorded and
photographed. The search warrant required
the careful measurements so that the exact
location from which seized items were taken
could be noted during a trial or other court
procedures.

After two days inside the emerald green

clapboard home, the investigative team hauled away about 50 boxes and bags of potential evidence containing nearly 100 items.

As Scott's anguished mother, Jackie, told reporters in San Diego, the search was part of a police campaign to harass her son, Modesto officials stuck to their original story that Laci's husband wasn't a suspect. Police media relations specialist Doug Ridenour explained that detectives "would like to eliminate Scott from the investigation."

Even so, police had already questioned or otherwise checked out about 200 registered sex offenders, the homeless, mentally ill, parolees and neighbors of Scott and Laci, as well as many people who were close to her. They were all eliminated as suspects. Even to the most casual observers it was looking more and more like Scott was illuminated smack in the middle of the investigator's spotlight.

Scott told MSNBC-TV that he hoped police were doing everything they could to find his wife. "I'm missing my wife and child," he said. "I can't sleep. Sometimes I feel I just can't do it. I feel like I'm in a dark corner and I just can't function."

There was no question that the pressure

was building on Scott, and he was drawing unwanted attention with his strange behavior.

He developed the disturbing habit of talking about his missing wife and unborn child in the past tense, as if he knew they were already dead.

"She was amazing," he said when talking to reporters. Then, recognizing the mistake, he quickly corrected himself. "She is amazing."

Chapter 11

SECRETS AND SWEET-TALK

Amber Frey was busy with her work and her daughter and didn't have much time for watching television or reading newspapers. The search for Laci was going on for almost a week before she inevitably learned that she had been deceived by the smooth-talking lady-killer who was now at the center of a high-profile murder investigation. It didn't take Amber's private investigator friend long to come up with something to show her — toward the end of December, Scott's picture was plastered all over the newspapers as Laci's disappearance began to make headlines throughout the country.

A short time later, on Dec. 30, Modesto homicide detectives were talking to Scott's secret lover. The badly shaken Amber had telephoned the police department and asked: "Why are TV shows carrying photos of Scott Peterson and talking about his missing wife? He's my boyfriend."

The gray-eyed beauty was stunned and her heartbreak was evident as she poured out the sad story of how she met and became enamored with Scott while the huckster was on a trip selling fertilizer. She made it clear that she had no idea when she and the handsome salesman were seeing each other that he was married.

Police immediately arranged a meeting and confirmed the Fresno-area masseuse's story when she voluntarily submitted to a polygraph test and passed. She further established her credibility by producing photographs of her and Scott together in intimate, loving poses. One of the pictures was taken while Scott clowned around with a Santa Claus hat on his head at the home of one of Amber's friends. An adoring Amber was perched appealingly on his knee — and he was deliberately leaning in close while brazenly fondling her bottom as the revealing picture was snapped.

The picture-taking continued after the couple left the friend's apartment about 1:30 a.m. and returned to Amber's home. A relaxed Scott took off his shiny gray tie and unbuttoned his shirt and the couple talked about their future together. Then, in her gleaming kitchen, Amber again sat tenderly on her boyfriend's lap while they smiled happily, cheek to cheek, for another romantic snapshot.

Now police were looking at snapshots that were proof positive that Scott was cheating on Laci. Their marriage wasn't the idyllic union that he had described to detectives after she vanished.

Detectives were even more intrigued when Amber revealed that Scott continued to romance her by phone after Laci's disappearance without letting on that he was the husband of the pregnant woman for whom every police agency in California and much of the rest of the nation was on the lookout.

Amber was so outraged by Scott's cruel deception that she allowed police to recruit her to act as a secret "double agent" to help prove that he was responsible for his wife's disappearance and bring him to justice. She agreed to continue accepting telephone calls from Scott and to string him along while police listened in and taped the conversations. Quietly, behind the scenes, the cat-and-mouse game began.

As her home phone became the investigator's clandestine link to Scott, the courageous woman was closely watched and protected. Incredibly, even as the massive hunt for Laci continued and police worked to firmly link Scott to her disappearance, he continued to bombard Amber with romantic phone calls. Some of the calls even came from Guadalajara, Mexico, while he was there for a sales conference.

"The cops were able to listen in as he sweet-talked her about marriage, offered her expensive presents and even a European vacation — and desperately tried to get her to meet with him," a source close to the investigation revealed.

Most importantly, detectives were able to pick up vital clues from the calls to Amber.

The sleuths fed her key questions to ask when he phoned. And through her, they were able to gauge Scott's demeanor at regular intervals, listen to the stories he was telling when his guard was down — and sense his growing desperation. In the early weeks of the investigation, they even used the calls to keep track of his whereabouts.

Finally, police fed Amber the bombshell question they wanted her to ask: Did he have anything to do with Laci's disappearance?

"There were a few moments of silence before Scott answered. Then he told Amber, 'I had nothing to do with it. We're trying to find her,' " an investigative insider revealed. "The tone of his voice meant more to detectives than the denial. He was shaky and unsure of himself for the first time since they started listening in to his conversations with Amber."

In the weeks ahead, Amber was coached to ask the same question in different ways. "Police didn't get the confession they hoped for," the source revealed. "But every time, Scott's tone was slightly less confident. It was the first indication that he might crack."

Amber had to walk a fine line, never agreeing to a reunion with Scott while simultaneously

Always smiling – Laci, cute as a button at 2, playing Modesto girl's softball at 6 and a beautiful sweet 16.

Most observers believed Laci and Scott (top) were the "perfect couple." The mom-to-be adored her nephew, Antonio Rocha (below left) and glowed after learning she was pregnant (below right).

MISSING

$500,000 REWARD
FOR INFORMATION LEADING
TO HER SAFE RETURN

$50,000 REWARD

FOR INFORMATION LEADING TO
THE LOCATION AND RECOVERY
OF HER BODY

For reward information, contact:
THE CAROLE SUND/CARRINGTON
MEMORIAL REWARD FOUNDATION
in Modesto, California at (209) 567-1059

Laci (Rocha) Peterson

27 years old	Had been 8 mos. pregnant
5' 1" tall	125 to 140 lbs.
Brown eyes & hair	Medium complexion

Laci's family and friends are pleading with anyone who may know *anything* about her disappearance, her whereabouts, or her fate to either call the Modesto Police Department at (209) 342-6166 or leave information on the Laci Peterson Web Site.

www.lacipeterson.com

Worst nightmare – friends and family of Laci Peterson never imagined her shining face would land on these "missing" posters, shown throughout the nation after her mysterious disappearance.

House of horrors – the three-bedroom home at 523 Covena Avenue in Modesto, where authorities believe Scott savagely murdered his pregnant wife.

A neighbor found Laci's golden retriever, McKenzie, wandering the neighborhood trailing his leash, contributing to fears the woman was kidnapped off the street.

Police investigators cordon off the crime scene and cart away evidence as they build their case against Scott. The philandering husband allegedly loaded his wife's body into his pickup truck and dumped it into the San Francisco Bay.

Ready for motherhood – Laci, eight months pregnant, had decorated a nursery in baby blue for son Conner, due Feb. 10, 2003.

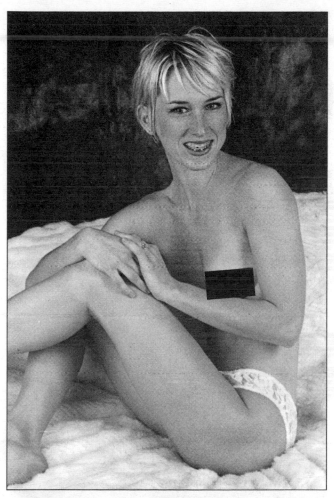

The other woman – Amber Frey, pictured here during a risque photo session, carried on a torrid affair with Scott.

Double life — Scott romanced Amber in Fresno as his pregnant wife waited to give birth 90 miles away in Modesto.

"I want us to be exclusive," Scott told Amber at a Christmas party they attended together (above). The scheming husband models a Santa hat and a cocky smile (left).

Divers comb the frigid waters of the Berkeley Marina, where Scott claims he went fishing for sturgeon on Christmas Eve.

Scott always asked volunteers to pray for Laci before leaving the search center at the Red Lion Inn with a handful of "missing" posters to distribute around town. "We found out later that what he was really doing was playing golf," revealed a neighbor.

Amber and Modesto authorities go public with the news of her and Scott's affair. Amazingly, he would continue to bombard the blonde with romantic calls, providing key evidence to police who taped every word.

"I trusted him and stood by him," Laci's brother Brent said at a press conference as evidence built against Scott. "Now I'm only left to question what he's hiding." Shown with him are Laci's mother, Sharon Rocha, and half-sister, Amy.

Scott Peterson looks on as police conduct a second search of his home. Investigators soon zeroed in on him as the prime suspect in his pregnant wife's disappearance.

"Awful, awful, awful," said a source about the condition of Laci's mutilated and decomposed body, which washed up on this beach in Richmond, Calif.

Authorities load Laci Peterson's body into a mortuary van on the banks of the San Francisco Bay. DNA testing positively identified the remains, as well as those of Conner, who washed up nearby a day earlier.

High-profile defense attorney Mark Geragos vowed to find "the person truly responsible" for murdering Laci, even as evidence mounted against his client, Scott Peterson.

Locked away – shackled and handcuffed, Scott Peterson is led into court to face homicide charges.

Ron Grantski and Sharon Rocha, seated, are comforted at the memorial service.

On April 27, 2003, the day Laci would have turned 28, thousands of strangers joined friends and family at the First Baptist Church in Modesto to attend a memorial for the slain woman and her unborn son, Conner.

keeping him interested so that he would continue the calls. And despite her heartbreak and frayed nerves, the brave woman went on with the carefully planned charade, even as fears for her safety grew by her family members and police.

Amber carried off her double agent role magnificently. While police listened, they were learning more and more about Scott, what he was doing every day — and how he was coping with the pressure they were putting on him during the investigation. Then came the triumphant evening when a nervous Amber got the results her handlers were hoping for.

"All Scott was interested in was romancing Amber," said the insider. "But gradually, gently, Amber brought the conversation back to the script. She probed him about Laci, got nothing, then later came back to the subject and probed him again and again."

At last, Amber's persistence paid off when Scott dramatically contradicted himself. Abandoning his former insistence that he knew nothing about Laci's disappearance, he blurted out: "I didn't do anything to Laci, but I know who did. Somebody else is involved, but I can't tell you who."

Scott had made a dynamite confession that directly refuted earlier statements he made to police and led a source close to the case to declare that "The Amber Tapes" would obviously play a "starring role" if Scott was charged and brought to trial in Laci's disappearance. It would be nearly impossible for him to explain away the confession he made to Amber that night.

"It's the smoking gun cops had worked so hard to find," revealed the source. "For the first time since Laci vanished, he was actually admitting knowledge of what had happened to her. The detectives who heard the recording all thought the same thing, 'If he knows about it, he's involved in it.'"

Scott's chilling disclosure also highlighted the potential danger of Amber's nail-biting role. "With Scott still free, her family was worried about the jeopardy Amber might have put herself in by cooperating with the police investigation," an insider said. "And when they heard about his confession, their immediate thought was, 'If he really has an accomplice, does he have the power to reach out and harm Amber?' "

A dramatic indication of the mounting police concern for the safety of their spy occurred when she and her 2-year-old daughter left Fresno for a brief vacation in Vero Beach, Florida.

Detective Jon Buehler, one of the lead investigators, actually drove the mother and daughter to the airport in San Jose and watched as they boarded the plane to make sure that they weren't alone to face Scott if he made an unexpected appearance. And unknown to Amber, she was watched around the clock while she relaxed at a seaside condominium in Vero Beach.

The vacation provided only a brief respite from the strain of the potentially dangerous role she was playing. When Amber returned home, there were new scares. By then, police had placed an electronic positioning device in Scott's new truck and one night the gadget indicated to horrified detectives that the vehicle — presumably driven by its owner — was only three blocks from Amber's home, according to the insider. "Fortunately, he kept driving, but it was a scary moment," the source said.

While most of the media were busy hanging around the search center hoping for informational handouts or waiting for police press conferences, a veteran team of investigative reporters for the *National Enquirer* was running down witnesses and people who knew Laci or Scott. One of the people the tabloid newshounds turned up was Amber Frey.

When the *Enquirer* attempted to confirm the information with law enforcement authorities, police decided to share the information with the rest of the media. Amber agreed to come to Modesto and appear at a press conference.

Before that could occur, police had another job to do: On the evening of the same day they learned the *Enquirer* knew about the secret witness, police called Laci's grief-stricken family together to tell them about Scott's girlfriend. Laci's mother, stepfather, brother and half-sister were present. Police were unable to contact her father in time for him to join the gathering. Scott's family in San Diego was not contacted.

Detectives told the somber relatives about Amber and backed up their painful revelation by producing four pictures of the Fresno mom and Scott together. At least one of the photos, which Amber had passed on to police, was stamped with a date that showed it was taken just days before Laci disappeared — when she had been led to believe he was on a business trip. Another showed Scott and Amber smiling and posing together in front of a Christmas tree topped with a silver star after attending a party at the Fresno home of one of her close friends. The couple had their arms around each other and their hands were clasped together in front of them.

"No one at the party had any idea that this charming guy had a wife — and a pregnant wife at that — just 90 miles north up Highway 99," an insider remarked.

None of Laci's family members recognized the leggy blonde in the photographs — but there was no question in their minds that it was the same man who had been playing the role of a grieving husband who was desperate to find his missing wife.

"They just gazed in shocked silence at the photo of the smiling couple," a family source revealed.

The police officers also told the family about the insurance policy taken out on Laci after she became pregnant.

Scott committed a monstrous deceit and the family was devastated. They realized they had been fed lies that encouraged false hope, even while others were facing the dreadful possibility that Laci would never be returned to them alive. The revelation about

Amber and the insurance policy made many wonder what else the silver-tongued pitch-man might be withholding or lying about.

The missing woman's loved ones had welcomed Scott into their family with open arms because he was the man their precious Laci loved. Then they loyally supported him throughout the agonizing ordeal of the search, steadfastly refusing to believe that he might have possessed the secret to her ominous disappearance — or that he would betray her with another woman while she was home waiting expectantly for their son to be born.

Early in the investigation, while discussing the rock-solid support for Scott from most of Laci's loved ones, Ron Grantski said, " In this family, we believe in loyalty. Until someone proves different to me, I'm standing by Scott."

Even as much as Grantski and most of the rest of the family wanted to believe in Scott, even then, suspicion was beginning to tickle Ron's consciousness. Laci was missing about 10 days or so when he confronted Scott and asked point-blank if he had a girlfriend. Scott vociferously denied there was any woman in his life except Laci and Ron took him at his word, family spokeswoman Kim Petersen said.

The only family member who apparently wasn't surprised was the man who missed the meeting — Laci's proudly devoted father, Dennis Rocha. He suspected for a long time that Scott knew more about her bewildering disappearance than he was revealing. Scott was too slick, too smooth and Dennis never had a good feeling about the man who married his precious daughter.

Dennis was a soft-spoken, practical man of the soil, more impressed by what people did and how they behaved than by what they said. He was also observant and paid attention to body language. "I always noticed he had this strange twitch in his lip," Dennis once told a friend about his disturbing son-in-law. "It seemed to me like the kind of twitch a crazy person has."

"Dennis even suspected that Scott might be having an affair with one of Laci's best girlfriends," revealed a source close to the case. He was so concerned that he called a friend who was a psychic and asked him to hold a photo of the young woman and feel the vibrations to determine if she was having an affair with Scott.

Laci's dad told another friend that Scott was controlling and demanding, the type who wanted his martini waiting and his dinner ready when he got home. "He won't take a police polygraph test and now he's hired a top criminal lawyer," Dennis is said to have additionally complained. "Scott won't look me in the face when he talks to me. He just stares down at the floor. I know in my heart he had something to do with my daughter's disappearance."

Dennis didn't learn about Scott's girlfriend until his distraught son, Brent, telephoned him and blurted out, "He didn't have to kill her!" the source disclosed.

The anguished dad, whose family came from Portugal, reportedly said he wished he could encourage Scott to talk by handling the matter "in the traditional Portuguese way — I'd take a knife and cut off his fingers, one by one, till he told me what happened."

Dennis deliberately kept a low profile during the search for his daughter because he was a man who admittedly showed his emotions and he was worried that he might say or do something that could cause problems for other family members or for investigators. But the big, bearded man's heart was breaking and he confided to a reporter that some days he felt like crouching in a corner and crying. He said he spent a lot of time in his game room that was filled with pictures of his missing daughter flashing her million-dollar smile. He simply couldn't understand why anyone would want to harm a person who was so nice.

Amber agreed to appear at a press conference at the Modesto Police Department on Jan. 24. Ridenour, the department's spokesman, began the widely televised meeting by reading a statement expressing police willingness to share information with the media that was significant and would not compromise the investigation.

The press flack announced that Amber would make a brief statement, but he said neither of them would answer questions. Police had also asked Amber not to talk to the media in the near future, he said. "It is her desire that you respect her privacy. Please don't follow, harass or make any attempts to interview her during this investigation."

Ridenour said Amber contacted Modesto Police on Dec. 30, then met with detectives and provided information about her relationship with Scott. She cooperated in the investigation, was not a suspect in Laci's disappearance and the information she provided was verified by a variety of means, the statement said.

Continuing to read from the statement, Ridenour pointed out that the pregnant woman was still missing. "Laci is described as 5'1", 140 pounds with brown shoulder-length hair and a sunflower tattoo on her left ankle," he said. "Laci was eight months pregnant and was last described as wearing a long-sleeve, white shirt and black pants. Her husband, Scott Peterson, last saw her on Dec. 24 at approximately 9:30 a.m."

Amber stood nearby, nervously waiting her turn to read a prepared statement when she was introduced. Tears flowed as she outlined her stunning confession and told the mass of reporters that she had no idea her boyfriend was married with a pregnant wife. Her voice shook as she spoke and at times she paused to take measured breaths before resuming.

"First of all, I met him on Nov. 20. When I was introduced, I was told he was not married. Scott told me he wasn't married," she declared. "We had a romantic relationship. When I discovered he was involved in the Laci Peterson case, I immediately contacted the Modesto Police Department."

The gray-eyed blonde added that she could

have sold the photos of her and Scott but didn't want to jeopardize the investigation. She said she knew that wasn't the right thing to do. She also expressed her sympathy for Laci's family and said she prayed for her return.

The single mother was a sympathetic figure and appeared to be just one more woman victimized by a straying husband with the inclinations and morals of a tomcat. Several of Laci's closest friends stood behind the row of TV cameras and audio equipment, quietly listening and watching.

Modesto Police Chief Roy Wasden described Amber as "a young woman who had the courage to come forward and give us information."

Amber's public persona as a wronged woman who was to be pitied for putting her trust in the wrong man and to be praised for her courageous undercover work in the police investigation was shaken when a treasure trove of nude pictures she posed for long before meeting Scott turned up. In October 1999, she answered a Fresno photographer's advertisement seeking models. She signed a release agreeing to pose nude, then stripped to her skivvies for topless — then even more daring — photographs.

While filling out the release she confirmed that she had no tattoos or body piercings and described her ambitions as: "to be successful, finish school, make lots of money." She wrote that her turn-ons were "smells." Her turnoffs were snooty people — misspelled on the form as "snoody peoples."

The photographer later recalled that Amber wasn't at all shy about exposing her body. "She obviously had a modeling career in mind, but strangely she never came back to collect the pictures or see the proofs," revealed the source.

Amber's reputation took a heavier hit later when a woman claimed that she was pregnant when Amber stole her husband and broke up her marriage.

"Amber is by no means the innocent she's portrayed herself to be," Michelle Hart told reporters.

"I was married and seven months pregnant and she ran off with my husband. Amber knew the whole time that my husband was married and that I was pregnant with our child," the Fresno mom of a 4-year-old son bitterly went on. "I pleaded with her to let him go, but it was no use."

The spurned wife added that she "just

about screamed at the television, 'this is b**l s**t!' " when she saw Amber "acting like the huge victim" and saying she would never have dated Scott if she knew he was married. Amber's television appearance made all the bad memories of their old conflict come flooding back, Michelle said.

She was pregnant about four years earlier when she started to have suspicions about her husband. "Then I heard a message a woman had left for him on voice mail," Michelle said. " She just gave her first name — Amber — and a number."

The pregnant woman dialed the number and was connected to Amber's phone at work. When she asked for Amber, Michelle said that a co-worker replied, "Oh, you mean Amber Frey."

Michelle was shocked and she confronted her husband, who, she said, at first denied being involved in an affair but eventually admitted it was true. He said he and Amber had met at a gym.

"He was so much under her spell that before I had the baby he moved in with Amber," the jilted wife recalled. She claimed her agony and humiliation was increased when she learned that Amber threw a baby shower and invited all her friends and co-workers. Michelle said Amber brazenly told them the shower was for the child of her boyfriend and his wife.

"Our child never saw any of the gifts — I wouldn't have wanted him to! But when Amber and my husband eventually split up a few months later, she told him that since all the shower gifts came from her friends she was keeping them for when she had a child of her own," the outraged wife added. "It was just insane!"

Michelle's little boy was born a month before the due date and the new mom blamed stress from her husband's flagrant love affair for the early arrival.

Michelle said that despite the disgraceful behavior of her husband and his mistress, she still wanted him back. And after her son was born healthy and beautiful, she decided to confront her rival in a desperate, final attempt to rescue her dreadfully maimed and crippled marriage. She selected a time when she knew her husband and Amber wouldn't be together and telephoned to arrange a meeting.

The wife and the mistress sat together in Michelle's car during the tense meeting.

Amber's hair was cut short and she had braces on her teeth, and when she mentioned she was considering enlisting in the Navy, Michelle almost had to bite her lip to keep from speaking out because she was thinking: "That would suit you. You look like a man!"

The new mother said she did everything but drop down on her knees to beg Amber to bow out of the tawdry romantic triangle. The heart-rending contest over Michelle's husband had turned into a torturous real-life soap opera, but she couldn't simply punch a button and switch it off.

"I pleaded with Amber to leave him alone. I remember crying, 'Please, please let him go. You keep making it harder for him to leave by making it easier for him to stay,' " Michelle recalled.

Amber asked about Michelle's relationship with her husband and the snubbed wife replied, "He's been part of my life the entire time he's been a part of your life."

As the conversation continued, Michelle's pain boiled to the surface and she said some admittedly nasty things about her husband and his cool brassy mistress. Amber had a tape recorder in her purse — and she later played the entire conversation back for the philandering husband, Michelle claimed. Later, he quoted every word to her that was said in the car that day.

But there was another ego-shattering surprise still to come. Months after Amber and her boyfriend split up, he and his wife reconciled and Michelle discovered a baby book he was keeping. He had recorded a visit to the hospital by Amber to see the little boy when he was only an hour old. The mother previously had no idea her husband's mistress had visited the hospital for a peek at his son.

"When I heard that, I just wanted to kill her," the outraged mom remembered.

The reconciliation didn't last long. After a few months the couple separated for good and they were eventually divorced. Still smarting over the demeaning experience, Michelle said she continued to believe that her marriage may have had a chance of succeeding without her husband's girlfriend.

"Amber has been pleading for sympathy over her involvement with Scott Peterson, but I've no sympathy for her," she declared. "She's manipulative and crazy."

When Michelle's former husband was located and asked about the affair, he claimed he was separated from his wife when he began dating Amber.

When it was publicly revealed Amber had been involved with a married man who had a pregnant wife at home, this time with murderous results, the father of the willowy blonde beauty contacted reporters and told them his daughter was completely fooled by the smooth-talking fertilizer salesman. Ron Frey said his daughter knew that it didn't pay to be around married men, Ron Frey said.

"But Scott fooled her — she had no clue in the world he was married. He said all the right things, that he wanted to be with her," Frey declared. "She was so proud of him — she thought he was real and that she had a future with him. What's happened since she learned the truth has broken her heart."

Amber not only convinced a nationwide TV audience of her innocent motives with her emotional confession, but she also won over most of Laci's family members and many of the missing woman's friends. After the TV appearance, many of them thanked her for coming forward, according to an informed source.

"Amber cried and assured them all that she'd never have gone out with Scott if she'd known he was a married man — and was horrified to learn his wife was pregnant," the tipster said. "They told her they supported her and thanked her."

Incredibly, even after police informed Laci's family about Scott's secret girlfriend and the insurance policy, he showed up the next morning at the volunteer center just as if nothing had happened. He appeared shocked when members of the family angrily confronted him and ordered him to leave.

After learning of Scott's deceit, the disheartened family announced that The Laci Peterson Volunteer Center, where news crews had taped film showing him helping run the massive private effort to find his wife, would be closed. After functioning for approximately three weeks as the hub for the search, it would never open again.

At an emotional, teary family news conference at the hotel command center, Laci's half-sister Amy was the first to step before the mass of reporters and the phalanx of microphones. All the family members looked drained and downcast and clearly showed their exhaustion. Amy struggled to force the words out and tears streamed down her cheeks as she described the past month as "the most painful time I've ever experienced." Then she broke down and was unable to continue.

Brent was the next to speak and he said he had confronted his brother-in-law about the affair with Amber and Scott admitted it. "I would like Scott to know I trusted him and stood by him in the initial phases of my sister's disappearance," Laci's shaken sibling said in a voice that trembled. "However, Scott has not been forthcoming with information regarding my sister's disappearance and I'm only left to question what he might be hiding." Brent added that because the family had so many questions about Scott, he could "no longer support him."

Brent said Laci's disappearance had completely changed his life, and speaking as if he was talking directly to her, he said he missed "your beautiful smile and your fun-loving personality."

"We talked about our children growing up together, spending summers at each other's house," he said, struggling to maintain his composure. "Family events will be very lonely without you and Conner. Wherever you may be, I hope you know how much I love you and how important you are to me. My search will never end."

Sharon also spoke, pleading for her daughter's return. "Since Christmas Eve, our one and only focus has been to find Laci and bring her home to us," she said. "I love my daughter and miss her every minute of every day. I miss seeing her. I miss our talks together. I miss listening to the excitement in her voice when she talks to me about her baby.

"I miss sharing our thoughts and our lives together. I miss her smile and her laughter and her sense of humor. I miss everything about her," the anguished mother went on. "Someone has taken all of this away from me and everyone else who loved her. There are no words that could possibly describe the ache in my heart and the emptiness in my life."

The family's shared pain hung over the quiet room like a shroud and their description of their loss was powerful and compellingly heartrending — even to veteran reporters who were no strangers to the grief of strangers. They were also misty-eyed and uncharacteristically quiet as Laci's relatives poured out their torment and misery.

Kim Petersen shared their worries and fears, but the spokeswoman was composed as she told reporters: "If Scott has nothing to hide, they ask that he prove it. He has continually allowed family members and friends to support him personally as well as on television." Kim said the family was also asking that people continue to search for Laci and especially appealed to farmers and others living in rural areas to look through their fields and barns. They asked that hunters, fishermen and even Realtors showing empty homes remain on the lookout.

Although Laci's family knew about Scott's deceit, he continued for a while to deny to outsiders that he had cheated on her or that he took out a big insurance policy on her the previous summer. "Well, it's a bunch of lies," he said in an interview. "So what are you to do? I'm going to come back to Modesto and open my own volunteer center and find my wife and kid."

He never did open the search center, but a short time later publicly admitted that he did cheat on Laci with Amber.

Scott's employers remained loyally in his corner, according to the *Modesto Bee*. Eric Van Innis, executive director of Tradecorp, met with his employee at his home after flying in from Portugal for a visit. Van Innis told reporters that he and the company supported Scott "100 percent" and described the young man as "doing his best."

One evening in late January, Scott's sister-in-law, Janey Peterson, made a series of telephone calls to national television networks defending him.

"There is absolutely no way Scott had anything to do with Laci's disappearance," she said in a call to CNN's *The Connie Chung Show*. Janey said that Laci didn't know about any affair, but that wasn't what really mattered, anyway. "It's a distraction from what our primary focus needs to be and that's to bring Laci home," she declared. "Scott's going to be OK at the end of this road, but we don't know that about Laci and that's where our focus needs to be."

The furor was devastating to the senior Petersons and to their large family, and their pain and suffering had been largely overlooked by much of the press and public. He was the baby of the family, had never been in trouble before and the Petersons rallied to his defense.

But they also loved Laci and had been looking forward to welcoming another grandchild into their growing family. Soon after Laci vanished, the Petersons traveled to Modesto to meet with her loved ones. After that, whenever any of Laci's folks appeared to publicly talk with the press, someone from Scott's family was almost always by their side.

Members of the two families appeared on CNN television's *Larry King Live* show on Jan. 13, along with several other guests including Marc Klaas, who became a victims' advocate after his 12-year-old daughter, Polly, was kidnapped from the bedroom of her home in Petaluma and murdered in 1993; Kim Petersen, the family spokeswoman and director of the Carole Sund/Carrington Memorial Reward Foundation; Court TV's Nancy Grace, a former prosecutor; Modesto Police Chief Roy Wasden, and big-time Los Angeles criminal defense attorney Mark Geragos — a program regular. Most of the guests were interviewed from other cities by video hookups during the call-in show.

Asked how Scott was holding up, his father, Lee, replied that he was devastated, terribly distraught and had lost weight. "I've never seen him so sad. He's just what you'd expect from someone who is missing their wife and baby," the distressed dad replied. "It's terrible to watch. I feel so bad. I wish I could help him."

Scott's sister-in-law Janey said they counted on family, friends and leaned on God to get through the ordeal.

In response to questions from the host, Lee Peterson and Sharon Rocha each described the marriage of their children as happy. "They just are really truly in love with each other," Sharon said. "They do everything together. They're partners. They're a team. They love each other. They planned together, they played together. They're always smiling. They're just a very happy, well-adjusted couple."

Asked why his son didn't do interviews, Lee replied that Scott was emotional and wouldn't be able to finish because he would break down. Then he echoed his son's frequent excuse for avoiding personal questions about his behavior and activities by remarking that Scott wanted to keep the focus on Laci and keep her face in front of the nation.

King asked Lee about reports that Scott may have mopped the kitchen floor, showered and changed clothes before calling for help. Scott said Laci was mopping the floor when he left the house, Lee replied.

The disclosure about Scott's cheating changed the relationship between the two families and after that there were no more joint appearances. The Petersons would continue to speak, but only from their home in southern California. The strain grew worse as Scott's image was publicly transformed from a grieving, concerned husband to that of an outrageous philanderer and liar — and the man who was widely suspected of being responsible for Laci's disappearance.

At their comfortable single-story home in the affluent San Elijo Hills neighborhood of Solano Beach, a note apparently handwritten by Lee Peterson was posted on the front door. "We will not talk to anyone. My wife is ill; you are contributing to that. Please respect our privacy," the note read. It also asked that any questions be directed to a family friend. The friend's name and telephone number were included on the message.

As investigators continued to ratchet up the pressure, the few people left to support Scott Peterson were jumping ship.

Chapter 12

THE NET CLOSES

By late February the number of tips and leads had swelled to more than 8,000, swamping civilians and officers from the Modesto Police Department and other law enforcement agencies working to check them all out. The calls ranged from the ridiculous, outrageous and bizarre to intriguing and potentially helpful.

Falling into the outrageous category was one tip indicating that despite Laci's advanced pregnancy, she may have been engaged in a torrid romantic fling with an old boyfriend. The suggestion was quickly discredited.

Another bizarre theory passed on to skeptical police suggested Laci may have been carrying a cloned baby. A UFO cult known as the Raelians was in the news at that time, with claims that one of their female members gave birth to a cloned infant. That Laci's disappearance might have been caused by any involvement with the cult, cloned babies or extraterrestrials was also promptly ruled out.

When one of the Peterson's Modesto neighbors complained that she wasn't contacted by investigators after calling in to report she saw Laci between 10 and 10:15 a.m. on Dec. 24, about 45 minutes past the time Scott claimed to have left on his fishing trip, overworked police acknowledged that they hadn't returned calls to everyone who phoned in tips.

About three weeks later, another Modesto woman claimed that police didn't respond to two calls she made to the tip line reporting she saw Scott at about 9:45 a.m. Christmas Eve when she stopped beside his truck at a red light. She said she motioned to Scott that something appeared to be coming loose from the bed of his truck and he peered at her through his side window, giving her "the most horrifying, scary look I have ever seen in my life."

Although police remained tight-lipped about who their primary suspect really was, it looked to many people like investigators were zeroing in on the missing woman's husband. As the days lengthened in to weeks and then months with no trace of Laci, it also appeared to even some of the most optimistic observers that the chances of a happy ending to the massive investigation and search were becoming increasingly slim.

Scott knew he was in the hot seat — caught like a deer in the headlights. And at last he began to work on damage control by making himself more available to a few carefully selected media outlets — especially the hosts of national television shows. He was angry over articles printed in the hometown *Modesto Bee* and let reporters from that publication know their chances of getting an interview were nonexistent.

But in an approximate one-week period, he answered questions on about a half-dozen TV shows — including a two-part videotaped interview for ABC Television's *Good Morning America* with co-host Diane Sawyer. Members of his family also participated in the program.

Many observers agreed that instead of

helping his case, Scott may have seriously damaged his image because of his unsettling behavior during the G.M.A. appearance. He was still having trouble remembering to talk of his missing wife and son in the present tense.

After describing his marriage as "glorious" — even though he admitted two-timing his pregnant wife — Scott remarked: "We took care of each other very well." He claimed his confession to Laci of an illicit liaison "wasn't anything that would break us apart."

As the show host looked on, seemingly sympathetic, he declared: "I had absolutely nothing to do with (Laci's) disappearance. It's turned on me because of the (affair) I had."

Scott denied that he took out a $250,000 insurance policy the previous summer after Laci learned she was pregnant. He claimed they each had $250,000 policies, both of which were taken out two years ago.

In an attempt to explain away blood found inside his pickup, Scott said that he frequently cut his hands while working at his job as a fertilizer salesman. There "would be plenty" of blood in the truck, he declared. Scott showed his hands, presumably so the interviewer could see the cuts and nicks. But when he was asked about the blood by an interviewer for a local TV outlet later that day, he changed his story. "I was reaching into my toolbox and cut my knuckle," he said. "There's a bloodstain on the door." Although the blood had been submitted to serology tests, and possibly to DNA testing, police still hadn't revealed whose it was — Scott's, Laci's or someone else's.

Scott's body language was troubling and, although tears emerged as he talked, somehow he managed to do his crying without losing his composure. Experts in interviewing and deception detection techniques are aware that grief is the most difficult emotion to fake. To some people at least, he came across during the interview not as a husband who was grieving for his lost wife and son, but as a man who was feeling a quite different emotion — fear.

One lie detection expert wrapped up his conclusions of Scott's performance on the TV talk show in the most blunt words possible. Scott, the expert declared, "lied through his teeth" when he said he didn't murder his wife.

"He's a classic deceiver and he's guilty as hell," declared Alfred Starewich, who scientifically analyzed stress levels in Scott's voice during the nationally televised interview.

Starewich said that Scott's deception levels were "off the charts" on all major points of the investigation into his wife's disappearance.

When Sawyer asked Scott if he murdered his wife, he replied, "No, no, I did not. And I had absolutely nothing to do with her disappearance." On that question alone, the husband showed extremely abnormal stress. "We call it a panic response," Starewich said.

The fertilizer salesman claimed he told police about his affair with Amber on Dec. 24, the day his wife vanished. But Starewich believed that was a lie. The expert also said Scott was lying when he denied there were other lovers he had been involved with.

The nation's leading voice stress analyst, Starewich is a former U. S. Marine counterintelligence agent and police chief. He has served as a consultant for the CIA, DEA, FBI and other law enforcement agencies around the world. He uses a high-tech psychological stress evaluator known as the Diogenes D6000P, an instrument that measures tremors in a person's vocal cords "triggered by the brain, where lies come from." Proponents of the device say it is far superior to a polygraph machine and never gives inconclusive results.

"Voice analyses are accepted as probable cause by judges for the purposes of issuing search warrants," Starewich pointed out after analyzing Scott's performance during the interview. "In my opinion, there is probable cause to arrest Scott Peterson."

As the interview continued, Sawyer asked Scott if he ever hit or injured his wife. "No, no. My God, no," he quickly replied. He went on to say, "Violence toward women is unapproachable. It's the most disgusting act to me."

Starewich said Scott's response revealed deception.

People generally close their eyes when they lie, the expert explained. And every time the voice analyzer showed deception on Scott's part, "he had his eyes closed when you looked at him being interviewed."

Scott did several other interviews at his home, sitting down to be grilled without the benefit of a lawyer present. More than a dozen TV trucks were parked outside the house, while inside he answered a barrage of questions that reporters had been itching to ask for weeks.

Sacramento TV-KOVR reporter Gloria Gomez asked Scott about his claim that he told his wife about his affair with Amber. "It was the right thing to do," he said of his motivation for the painful confession. "And, as you know, when you're not doing the right thing, it eats you up. You know you feel sick to your stomach and you can't function. And you have a hard time, you know, looking at someone."

Scott also told a TV interviewer that he had spoken to Marc Klaas. But the missing children's advocate told Fox News' Greta Van Susteren that he never talked with Laci's husband.

There was a lot of room for suspicion in Scott's demeanor and his performance was clumsy before the TV cameras, but it isn't a capital crime to come across as less than perfect when the lights are shining on you and a skeptical reporter or host is breathing down your neck. Scott was a fertilizer salesman, after all, and not a windy politician or a smooth, perfectly groomed and practiced talking head.

Scott soon had more to worry about than his TV persona. Trouble came at him from all sides and it was disclosed that he had been discussed in relation to the unsolved disappearances of at least three other young women in California. One of them was pregnant when she vanished.

"Anyone who can do what Scott is charged

with has the personality type to have killed before," former FBI special agent-in-charge Ted Gunderson explained in an interview with the press. "We know that he has traveled to numerous cities in California. Police departments are no doubt sharing information about unsolved homicides where there would be a Peterson link."

Kristin Smart was a gorgeous 19-year-old coed at Cal Poly on May 25, 1996, when she disappeared. Scott was also a student there at the time, but there was no proof that he dated Kristin — or even knew her. An anonymous letter was mailed to the local newspaper, the *Telegraph and Tribune*, shortly after the disappearance, claiming that the leggy 6-foot-1-inch blonde's body was dumped in nearby Lopez Lake. But the young woman from Stockton, California, has never been found.

According to investigators, she was last seen walking back to her dorm room at about 2 a.m. with Paul Flores, another freshman. It was three days before her roommates reported her missing. No one was ever arrested in the baffling case.

San Luis Obispo County Sheriff's Lieutenant Steve Bolts confirmed to a reporter that investigators were looking at

Scott's class schedules to try and figure out if the two students ever crossed paths. The lieutenant said investigators talked with hundreds of people as part of their investigation into the college girl's mysterious disappearance and Scott's name was in the case file as one of those apparently slated for contact. But police couldn't find any evidence that Scott was actually interviewed. A letter requesting information was sent to hundreds of students, including Scott, but he never returned it, the officer indicated.

The victim's mother, Denise, told another reporter that the FBI wanted to interview Scott at the time but he never came forward for questioning. "I need to know why he was on that list — what connection he had with my daughter," she declared. Denise said she wanted him thoroughly investigated by police for any connection with Kristin's disappearance. The 55-year-old woman also said she was contacted by someone who claimed her daughter and Scott had dated.

"Even if he wasn't involved with Kristin's disappearance, maybe Scott saw the real culprit literally get away with murder and decided he could do the same thing himself," the grieving mom surmised.

Kristen Modafferi, another pretty coed from North Carolina with an almost identical first name except for the spelling, was taking summer photography classes at the University of California-Berkeley when she vanished on June 23, 1997. The 18-year-old brown-eyed, brown-haired beauty was last seen in the Lands End area of San Francisco near the Marina where Scott said he was fishing when his wife vanished. Kristen had shoulder-length hair and big, deep-set dimples in her cheeks — like Laci.

Also like Laci, 24-year-old Evelyn Hernandez was pregnant when she and her 5-year-old son, Alex, dropped from sight on May 1, 2002. She was missing more than a year before her headless body was recovered in San Francisco Bay on July 24, 2002. Alex was never found.

Police suspected that Evelyn wasn't the only pregnant woman to be dumped in the chilly waters of San Francisco Bay. Gene Ralston of Ralston and Associates was hired by the Modesto Police Department to search the waters with side-scan sonar, technically sophisticated equipment that picks up three-dimensional images that are clearer than those found through the use of regular sonar. When he contracted for the job, he was told not to be surprised if he found a lot of bodies. The San Francisco Bay is a popular dumping ground for murder victims and people who die of drug overdoses or in other circumstances that might threaten the freedom of their family members or associates. Suicides also regularly account for "floaters" and for other bodies that sink or are snagged in debris and mud at the bottom. San Mateo County Sheriff's Department deputies also volunteered their help and joined in the search with their own expensive side-scan sonar that, like Ralston's, is capable of covering large areas more rapidly than the less sophisticated equipment.

A flurry of activity was ignited when an early sonar scan by the San Mateo county team picked up a suspicious image on the floor of the bay in the area of the Berkeley Marina early on a Thursday evening toward the end of January. When the object was first sighted, exhausted divers had already been scanning the chilly waters for days. As a storm rolled in, the recovery effort was postponed until the weather cleared.

About 36 hours later, at dawn on Saturday morning, more than 90 officers from several law enforcement and search and rescue departments, including Modesto police, gathered at the marina to resume the search and recover the mystery object. The somber officers and civilians were apprehensive and two people from the Stanislaus County District Attorney's Office were present at the search scene in case the fears were justified.

Seven small boats and a U. S. Coast Guard cutter made up the tiny armada assembled to carry out the search. An Alameda County search and rescue team loaded a basket stretcher onto one of the boats. The stretcher would be needed if the divers brought up Laci and her baby.

A search zone more than two miles off shore and covering about 2,200 square feet, 300 yards west of the end of the old Berkeley pier, was established and a half-dozen buoys were set out to mark the perimeter. Fishermen and pleasure boaters were barred from the area.

Divers used the Coast Guard vessel as a platform to plunge into the bay and carry out a meticulous search, feeling along the muddy bottom with their hands because the murky water was too gloomy and dark to see through. It was 11:45 a.m. before the first diver splashed into the water, one of 12 who worked in 20-minute shifts. They located what they believed to be the same object spotted Thursday using the side sonar north of the Bay Bridge near the Berkeley Pier. It proved to be nothing but an old anchor. San Francisco Bay is littered with such objects — chunks of old ships and all kinds of ancient jetsam — some of it going back to the San Francisco area's Gold Rush days.

About 1 p.m. word reached Modesto that the mystery object wasn't a body as suspected and the disclosure led to cheers and applause among civilian search volunteers and family members who had been waiting in dread. Everyone wanted the exhausting search to end — but not that way. They wanted Laci and her baby alive and healthy, back with her loved ones where she belonged.

A couple of hours later, Modesto Police Sergeant Ron Cloward, who was in charge of the bay search, made it official. "We have concluded the search today of the Berkeley Marina," he announced to a swarm of reporters at 3:20 p.m. "The dive team located an anchor sunk down in the bottom of the bay. It was removed." Cloward explained the delay in making the announcement by pointing out that the search team wanted to make sure the anchor was the only object the sonar hit had detected. When the area was rechecked, nothing showed up.

The only thing search teams had turned up during the first couple of weeks around the marina was a piece of tarpaulin pulled from the water on Jan. 4, the first day the waters around the marina were scanned. It was found in the same area that later produced the sunken anchor. Cloward described the tarp to reporters as "nothing significant," but it was kept for examination.

No one wanted to look at the conclusion as a disappointment, but the longer the search dragged on the dreadful forebodings increased and if the vibrant young woman was dead, law enforcement authorities desperately wanted to locate and recover her body. Only then would her family have an opportunity to deal with final arrangements, including proper burial and begin to rebuild their lives. And if she was determined to be a homicide victim, as was widely feared, law enforcement authorities would be a giant step closer to capturing the killer and bringing him or her to justice.

The absence of a body did not mean that other evidence wouldn't be sufficient to arrest and convict a suspect in her slaying.

But it would be important for prosecutors to show in court that she would not have vanished without good reason. Modesto police made it clear early in the case that they had no reason to suspect that the pregnant mother may have rambled off somewhere on her own. She was too close to her family and already too devoted to her lovingly anticipated baby boy to do something like that. Dropping out and cutting off all ties with family and friends simply wasn't Laci's style.

Famed O.J. Simpson prosecutor Marcia Clark once won a murder conviction in Los Angeles without the body of the victim. She got the job done with a single spot of blood that she used to illustrate its unique genetic pattern and match it to close family members of the victim. The blood spot was lifted from the rear passenger seat of a car the suspect was driving when arrested.

A handful of other murder cases in California have also been successfully prosecuted without bodies of the victims. In July 2000, Adolfo Romo Martinez was convicted by a Merced county jury of murdering Lilia Anguiano of Los Banos. Neighbors testified they saw the pair together shortly before the woman vanished. Her body still hasn't been found. And in 1982, Mark Christopher Crew shot and dismembered his wife, then dumped the body parts off the Dumbarton Bridge on San Francisco Bay after cleaning out her life savings, according to the *Modesto Bee*. He was sentenced to execution and was locked up on death row at California's notorious old San Quentin Prison.

Stanislaus county prosecutors had been faced at least a couple of times in recent history with the challenge of building cases against suspects without the discovery of a victim's body, but developments intervened to change the picture before prosecutors brought them to trial. They were working to put together a murder case against a suspect in the slaying of 69-year-old Joy Bell Goad in 1991, when her remains were finally found buried in her backyard. Her grandnephew had killed the woman with a roofer's hammer and was on the run until 1996. He was convicted of murder the following year.

More recently, in 2001, investigators were closing in on 61-year-old James Young and had scheduled him for a lie detector test as part of their probe into the disappearance of his girlfriend, Shanti Prakash, when he killed himself at Lake Tahoe. The woman's remains were discovered by hikers near the famous lake on the border of California and Nevada about eight months later.

No one at the Stanislaus County Prosecutor's Office in Modesto wanted to be in a position where they had to hope for a lucky break like those that occurred in the Goad and Prakash cases. And they weren't looking forward to trying to match Clark's accomplishment by winning a homicide trial without a body. If there was a body in the bay — or hidden anywhere else — law enforcement authorities were determined to find and recover it.

In mid-March, according to the *Modesto Bee*, Ralston picked up another promising hit while searching the Point Richmond area of the bay. His sonar detected a body, a barrel or some other unknown but intriguing object on the bottom. But nothing was recovered and police called off the hunt for the time being — but widespread suspicions continued to plague investigators, who were convinced the answer to the mystery was still resting somewhere at the bottom of the San Francisco Bay.

Chapter 13

A HOMICIDE CASE

On March 5, 2003, slightly more than nine weeks after Ron Grantski reported that his pregnant stepdaughter had mysteriously disappeared, police reclassified the investigation from a missing person case to a homicide case.

"As the investigation has progressed, we have increasingly come to believe that Laci Peterson is the victim of a violent crime," lead investigator Detective Craig Grogan announced.

The move had important implications — and repercussions.

Scott's mother Jackie strongly protested the reclassification and charged that it would keep people from continuing the search for her daughter-in-law, according to the *Modesto Bee*. She said it was sad because police treated the investigation as a homicide case from the beginning and officially labeling it as a murder probe took away hope.

Police spokesman Ridenour responded by explaining that officials realized that some family members may not understand the decision, but added: "It's difficult because they don't know everything investigators know." He also observed that the police department had already spent more than $250,000 on overtime pay for employees, which probably made it the most expensive investigation in the city's history. And the missing woman still hadn't been found.

Modesto's outspoken Mayor Carmen Sabatino stirred up a minor local political flap when he was quoted in *The New York Times* as saying the police department spent so much more on the Laci Peterson case than similar investigations because of the media. "We have spent the money on Laci because of the media," he said. "It is not the city that determines what the media considers a story." He added that the point of diminishing returns had been reached, but complained that authorities couldn't "turn off the faucet" while the press was still around.

It's unlikely that Scott was concerned about taxpayer money streaming out, but he must have wondered what was behind the reclassification. Certainly police would not have made the announcement unless they had important evidence that convinced them Laci wasn't merely missing — but that she and her baby, Conner, were dead.

One lead detective, who wasn't named by reporters, made this observation: "What the district attorney is telling us is (that) he's ready to go forward," the sleuth declared, "whether we have a body or not."

For the most part, police were staying tight-lipped, but speculation was widespread that the serology tests on the blood found in Scott's pickup truck had shown it came from Laci, not from her husband.

Detectives also had another chilling piece

of physical evidence they weren't publicly disclosing that neatly fit into the matrix they were molding to pin Scott to the ghastly crime. A pair of needle-nose pliers was found under one of the seats of his 14-foot aluminum boat and forensics tests disclosed that strands of hair still caught in its jaws were likely from his pregnant wife, Laci.

"They were pointy, needle-nose pliers and police believe Laci's hair got caught in them while Scott was preparing her body for disposal in San Francisco Bay," a source close to the family revealed. "He can't account for half of a roll of chicken wire he owned. He may have used the wire to wrap around Laci's body and cut or knot it with the pliers. That could be when her hair got caught in it."

With reclassification of the case to murder, the already intense heat on Scott was turned up a notch. Investigators were able to get him to come into police headquarters voluntarily to provide hair and blood samples, but once he was in the headquarters, a detective cornered him and began an interrogation, bombarding him with certain questions, according to an insider. "Scott wouldn't talk and later complained to his lawyer," the source said. "But cops had kept him on edge."

Yet another series of search warrants were obtained. One permitted police to open and inspect the contents of an envelope found in one of his vehicles and the other was for a unit at Security Public Storage — which was several blocks from the warehouse he used for his business. Police didn't disclose what they expected to find or what — if anything — was actually discovered.

Sometimes it seemed almost like the fates themselves were conspiring to give Scott the jitters. In mid-January, a woman he had trusted to walk Laci's dog, McKenzie, entered the house while he was away.

"She had a police record and when she broke into Scott's house, she took out Laci's wedding dress, got really drunk and then stole family photos and clothing," an insider disclosed.

Someone else apparently had it in for Scott and rammed a car or truck into the door of his combination office and warehouse. He discovered the vandalism and notified the Stanislaus County Sheriff's Department, which had jurisdiction because the Emerald Avenue building was in an unincorporated area at the western edge of the city. Sheriff's department investigators said the damage appeared to have been deliberate because of the angle from which the vehicle struck the door.

Scott clearly wasn't Modesto's most popular citizen, and the young man showed the effects of the mounting stress. He had lost about 25 pounds. According to his father, Scott had been "virtually homeless" since police tore his home apart during the second search of the house on Covena Avenue. Reporters were making matters worse by dogging his tracks every time he showed his face. Loss of his vehicles and computers to police was also making it difficult for Scott to perform his work and hang onto his job, the concerned dad indicated.

Ironically, Scott wasn't the only one stressed out by the national uproar over his wife's disappearance. The burglars who hauled the safe away from the neighbor's house, along with several shady characters who wound up with the stolen property, were also burned by the blistering heat generated by the search for Laci and the sweeping police investigation.

Police assigned two detectives full time to the burglary because they were concerned there might be a connection to Laci's disappearance. But they quickly determined that the break-in occurred on the morning of Dec. 26, about a day-and-a-half after she was reported missing and, early in the new year, police made two arrests in the case. State parole officers had received a tip from an unidentified informant, who led police to the suspects. The men taken into custody were especially cooperative because they wanted to do everything they could to clear themselves as possible suspects in Laci's disappearance, investigators revealed. The accused burglars said they were cruising the neighborhood about 4:30 a.m., when they spotted a house that looked empty and, even though several TV trucks were parked nearby, they broke in and carried the safe out the front door onto the lawn.

Late one night, about the time the frightened suspects were telling their story to detectives, another visibly nervous man walked into the police department, plopped a heavy duffle bag on the counter and told a cop that it was full of stolen property. Before the startled officer could summon someone to make out a report, the jittery stranger turned and ran outside.

The duffle bag was full of property taken in

the burglary near the Peterson home and its unexpected return likely had a lot to do with Police Sergeant Ron Cloward, one of the leading investigators involved in the search for Laci. Cloward hung around southeast Modesto, passing around his business cards and pointing out to some of the people known for handling stolen property that if they had any of the loot from the burglary they could avoid prosecution by returning it. A few days later, almost everything that was taken had been recovered by authorities.

Scott had enough to worry about without concerning himself over the burglary of his neighbor's home or return of the stolen property. His own house had been cleared out by police, was besieged by gawkers, troublesome journalists and tourists with nothing better to do, all of which made it almost impossible for him to continue living there. He spent less and less time in the home, until he moved out altogether. A sympathetic neighbor mowed the lawn for a while and then quit after Scott's deceitful philandering was exposed and he began to look increasingly like a suspect in his wife's disappearance, rather than the tormented, fretful husband of a missing wife.

A big banner with a picture of Laci that

included a plea for information and offering a $500,000 reward still slumped forlornly in the front yard. Sympathetic strangers were building their own impromptu shrine in front of the banner and it was growing every day with single roses, bouquets, yellow and blue ribbons, candles, teddy bears, keepsakes and envelopes with hand-scribbled notes promising continued love and prayers.

Early in the investigation, Scott occasionally stayed with friends, but more recently he spent more time in the comforting and familiar surroundings of San Diego.

Until the horror of Laci's mysterious abduction descended on the Rochas, the Petersons and the Grantskis, Scott had known little about how police worked and what techniques they used when they conducted a serious criminal investigation. The young man was so unsophisticated in the ways of law enforcement that he reacted to the psychological campaign and troubling intrusion into his life by making one stupid mistake after another.

After Scott's white pickup was returned to him by police during the second search of the house, his lawyer suggested that he have it checked over because the cops may have outfitted it with a locator device. But Scott was busy with his work and preoccupied with the furor over his missing wife and didn't get around to following his lawyers advice for a few weeks. When he finally had the truck checked, the mechanics found a bug. His lawyer was right all along and Scott must have been shocked when he belatedly realized that with every gallon of gas he poured into his tank and burned in the pickup, he was making it easier for police to stay solidly on his tail.

Scott's family was also reeling under the pressure and they were desperate to help prove his innocence in the increasingly ominous disappearance of his wife. His mother, Jackie, hired a nationally renowned psychic to hunt for her daughter-in-law. By that time, the number of tips and potential leads reported to police included about 300 from psychics.

It isn't unusual for people to look for help from psychics, spiritualist mediums or necromancers in time of trouble or great need. Biblical patriarchs, powerful kings, conquerors and political leaders have consulted such sources for thousands of years. Winston Churchill was a believer and the life of Great

Britain's World War II prime minister was saved at least twice by uncanny premonitions attributed to his amazing psychic abilities. Canada's World War II prime minister, MacKenzie King, consulted with his departed mother and a grandfather through mediums. And famed U.S. tank General "Old Blood and Guts" George S. Patton believed strongly in reincarnation and contact with the psychic world. Even President Franklin D. Roosevelt consulted an old black woman psychic known as Aunt Jane during WWII, but the public didn't learn about the secret meetings until long after FDR's death.

Like doctors and lawyers or just about any professionals, some psychics are better than others. Noreen Renier is one of the best and is highly respected in law enforcement circles for her no-nonsense approach to her work — and for her results. The attractive, dark-haired woman, who has assisted police in 38 states and lectured at the FBI Academy, spent hours on the Laci Peterson case.

Sensitives, as Renier describes herself, use a variety of means to peer into the future and the past. Some, like shamans in various parts of the world, use trance to induce visions. Others peer into crystal balls and magic mirrors or, in the age-old manner of mediums and necromancers, consult with the spirits of the dead.

Renier employed a different technique, psychometry, which is favored by a majority of the handful of successful psychics who work closely with police. Psychometry is sometimes called object reading because psychics who employ this method in their work receive extrasensory impressions from objects. Renier used some of Laci's personal items, which Jackie sent to her at the psychic's request. They included a Tommy Hilfiger shoe, size 6 medium, and a navy blue sweatshirt, size small, with the logo of Laci's college — Cal Poly San Luis Obispo — on the front. The psychometrist touched and ran her hands over the shoes and the shirt.

Renier's technique to obtain impressions and information goes a step or two further than some psychometrists. During her work sessions, she was guided by parapsychologist Dr. Joanne McMahon. As Renier went into a near-trance, she assumed the identities of both Laci and of her killer to make a number of shocking discoveries.

Scott, of course, had told police and others that when he left his house about 9:30 a.m.

on Christmas Eve to fish in San Francisco Bay for sturgeon, Laci was preparing to walk the dog.

But in taped transcripts of Renier's psychic sessions, after she assumed the identity of Laci, she suddenly told Dr. McMahon: "I am in a vehicle. I back out of the driveway. I feel a laying down and being put in (to the vehicle)." Renier revealed that she was concealed under a rug or cloth. Then the amazing clairvoyant said, "I'm already dead."

"You're dead when you're in the vehicle?" her guide probed, in order to clarify the statement.

"Yes," Renier confirmed. "It's late. Late at night or going into the early morning."

Further into the bone-chilling session, the psychic appeared to merge into the person of the driver — and said: "I'm putting her into the water with cement. It's around her. It's for her to sink."

As Renier returned — in spirit — to the Peterson house, where cops believe Laci was killed, she saw the murder weapon. It could be a club or a bat. "It is something you can hold in your hand and hit a person on the head," she said.

But most disturbing of all is the psychic's eerie depiction of Laci lying beneath water.

"It has a fishy odor," said Renier, who then described a grisly underwater tomb. "I think I am at the bottom. I'm stationary ... the water rushing past me."

In March, Renier e-mailed her report to Jackie, who never acknowledged it. But even without a client, the clairvoyant found she couldn't drop the case and held two more sessions that were never reported to the Petersons.

In the final session, on March 27 — aided by a second psychic guide, Sheri Enzor — Renier identified once again with Laci.

"We had an argument," she suddenly revealed. "I was going out and we had an argument, there was pushing and yelling. He does have a temper — most of the time controlled."

Renier's revelations were so disturbing that, in the end, she and Dr. McMahon felt compelled to send copies of her bombshell report to detectives. But when the psychometrist telephoned the woman who hired her, she was confronted with a puzzling reception. "I told Mrs. Peterson that as a matter of routine I would also be sending the report to the police in Modesto," Renier confided. "She seemed very nervous — then, very abruptly, she told me her attorney didn't want me to do that. Her attitude seemed to have changed since she hired me. She was a good deal less friendly."

Jackie's surprising about-face came as suspicion fell increasingly on her son, Scott.

"They (the authorities) are in possession of everything I've done," Renier added. "I just pray it helps them solve this awful crime."

After Renier failed to give Jackie Peterson the results she wanted, Scott's mother contacted the *Modesto Bee* and said she had believed from the beginning that Laci was kidnapped for her baby. While working at the volunteer center, Jackie received e-mails from two men who reported their pregnant wives were kidnapped, she claimed. Scott's mother said she also learned of three other similar abductions in the Bay Area and another in Fresno. All the e-mail tips were turned over to Modesto police.

The idea of an abduction to steal a baby about to be born was an intriguing theory. Even with several weeks to go before Laci was expected to give birth, she could have been held somewhere for a while — or an abductor could have performed his or her own crude Caesarean right away and taken the baby.

As awful as it is, that sort of thing happens. Every so often an expectant mom is killed by someone who wants her baby — usually a childless woman who is so obsessive about becoming a mother that she sets up the kidnap murder. Often she talks a male accessory into helping out.

One of the worst recent instances of murdering an expectant mother to take her unborn child occurred in Kent, Ohio, when 23-year-old Theresa Andrews was abducted Sept. 27, 2000, by a woman she met a few weeks earlier while shopping at a Wal-Mart for baby clothes. Michelle Bica shot her in the back, then carved the baby out of her stomach. A few days later, the 39-year-old Bica committed suicide in her bedroom when police showed up to question her. Another similar case occurred in Chicago, where a pregnant woman was followed to her home and killed by a couple who stole her unborn baby.

But detectives probing Laci's disappearance hadn't turned up any indication that she was abducted by someone intent on stealing her unborn son. It was true that investigators thought she was murdered, but they believed there was a different motive, and they didn't believe Laci's killer was a stranger. They were focusing their investigation on a suspect who was much closer to home.

Whether it was realization of Jackie Peterson's fears that reclassification of the investigation as a homicide would prevent people from continuing to search or if it was simply because everyone was simply worn out and couldn't think of new places to look for Laci, the number of calls to the tip line was rapidly dwindling.

Some of the flurry and fuss may also have been dying down because Scott had adopted a much lower profile and virtually dropped from public sight. Although he had already traveled to Guadalajara for the agriculture conference and returned to California, rumors were rife that he had fled or was about to flee the country to hide out in Mexico, Central or South America — or somewhere else.

Law enforcement officers knew that Scott wasn't in Mexico or in any other foreign country. They knew that he was right back home in California, often in the San Diego area, because they had secretly attached a locator device to his vehicle and were virtually dogging his every step. Amber also continued to work closely with detectives by accepting his calls and talking with him by phone, while investigators listened in and recorded everything on tape.

Public involvement in the race to find Laci was continuing to dwindle rapidly and from 8,000 calls recorded by the tips line through late February, the count rose by only about 900 through mid-April. But harried police were on the verge of getting the break they had been waiting for.

Chapter 14

BODIES

On Sunday afternoon, April 13, the wrinkled, waterlogged body of a fully-developed baby boy was discovered lying in a patch of grass along the shoreline of San Francisco Bay in south Richmond by a couple walking their dog. The infant washed ashore about three miles from the Berkeley Marina and his umbilical cord was still attached.

A few minutes before noon the next day, a woman who was also walking her dog along the edge of the East Bay discovered the ghastly remains of an adult Caucasian female lodged in a pile of rocks at the rugged

Point Isabel Regional Shoreline about a mile south of where the baby's body was found. The cadaver was discovered in marshy wetlands about 15 feet from the waterline in an area bordered by factories and condominiums, not far from where the headless body of the pregnant Hernandez woman washed up nearly nine months earlier. Detective Sgt. Cloward had crisscrossed the area in a helicopter during one of the searches because the water was only about 5 or 6 feet deep, too shallow for the type of boats and other equipment being used, but nothing unusual was observed.

By 5 p.m. Monday, April 14, the Modesto Police Department, the Stanislaus Sheriff's Department and the Stanislaus County District Attorney's Office had five people at the scene. The total number of investigators, including park police and canine teams from the local bay area Contra Costa County Sheriff's Department, quickly swelled to about 20.

At that point, the investigation was officially the responsibility of the park district police department because the bodies of the woman and the child were found in its area of jurisdiction. No one was saying so publicly, but there were probably few people, if there were any at all, who expected that situation to continue for very long.

Laci's family was notified before an official announcement was made and told that the body of a petite woman had been found along the shoreline of San Francisco Bay. A short time later, friends and neighbors of Laci and other people all over California and much of the rest of the nation watched in despair as images flashed on TV screens showing husky men in Contra Costa County carrying a body bag and loading it into a white coroner's van parked before the shimmering waters of the San Francisco Bay.

If the body turned out to be Laci, as most people involved in the investigation feared, it would be deplorably ironic because the day she was found was the birthday of another famous murder victim from Modesto — Chandra Levy. Chandra would have turned 26 years old.

Laci's loved ones had been through dreadful trauma already, but they were still reluctant to jump to conclusions and concede that the badly decomposed corpses that washed up along the bay were their missing relatives. In Escalon, Laci's father Dennis told a reporter from the *Modesto Bee* that it might be just "another wild-goose chase." Sharon and her husband, Ron, weren't talking about the discovery to reporters, and placed a sign on their front door asking reporters to contact Kim Petersen for information. But the spokeswoman had nothing to say for the time being, either. The family eventually released a short statement pointing out the obvious: The two bodies could potentially be their loved ones or they could belong to some other family "experiencing our same pain."

In San Diego, Jackie Peterson said she spoke with her son and they were praying the body of the woman wasn't Laci.

By necessity, authorities weren't disclosing many details about the rapidly mushrooming probe, but they shared what information they could. Park District Police Chief Norman Lapera revealed that the body of the woman appeared to have been in the water for quite some time, but he was unable to provide other specifics about its condition. Jimmy Lee, a spokesman for the Contra Costa County Sheriff's Department, the county in which the remains were found, said it was too early to determine if the body of the woman and the baby were in the water for the same length of time. A forensic anthropologist, whose specialty is submerged bodies, was eventually called in to try and determine how long the woman and the infant were under water and what happened to them there. Modesto police also called on the San Francisco medical examiner's office to advise them in the inquiry.

Lee confirmed that some clothing found with the woman's body was being examined.

An autopsy on the baby, which authorities described as a "full-term male child," was conducted Monday morning at the Contra Costa County Coroner's Office in Martinez. About 6 p.m. the same day, forensic pathologists in Martinez began an autopsy on the body of the woman. The macabre but matter-of-fact quest by pathologists to unlock the mysteries concealed by the clammy, gray flesh continued on into Monday night while two detectives observed the process.

Neither of the autopsies yielded an immediate answer to the mystery of the deaths. Lee said it could be several days before information was processed to determine the cause of death and identify the body.

Hair, tissue and bone samples were taken and specimens sent to the California

Department of Justice DNA Laboratory in Richmond for tests. Technicians at the laboratory were provided with a tibia, the largest of the two bones in the lower leg, from the woman's remains. A thigh bone, or femur, was provided from the baby. Lab technicians weren't immediately certain that usable DNA samples could be obtained from the adult body, because of its poor condition. If the samples were usable, as was hoped, they would be compared with DNA provided by members of Laci's family to see if there was a match. The technicians had a hair sample taken from Laci's hairbrush and inner-cheek saliva swabs from her parents to work with. They also had the blood samples previously taken from Scott.

Lone bones from the arms and legs and dental records often provide some of the most reliable elements for identifying bodies. When Lee was asked by reporters if dental records were part of the process for identifying the woman's body, he declined to comment.

There was sufficient intact DNA from the baby to make comparisons with the body of the woman to determine if they were related, laboratory authorities confirmed. Lee said that determining or ruling out a relationship between the two bodies was the key question medical and scientific professionals were working to answer at that time. News reporters were told it might be weeks before results of the laboratory analyses were known.

In Modesto, Stanislaus County District Attorney James Brazelton told reporters he felt "pretty strongly" that the woman found along the shoreline of San Francisco Bay was Laci. It was too much of a coincidence to find a woman and a baby close to each other only a day apart, when no others were known to be missing. "If I were a betting man, I'd put money on it," he was quoted as saying. Whether he may have gotten cold feet and was worried about stirring up a legal hornet's nest by jumping the gun or if it was merely normal prosecutorial caution, a few hours later Brazelton announced in a news release that the DA's office would no longer comment on the Peterson case.

There seemed to be little question, however, that almost everyone who was involved in the probe, or observing developments through reports in the press, believed that the bodies were Laci and Conner. During an afternoon press conference, John Tonkyn, supervisor of the missing person DNA program at the laboratory in Richmond, echoed that sentiment. "To date, we don't have another person in mind," he said of speculation that the adult woman was Laci.

Police simply couldn't reveal everything that was going on, but that left the rumor mill to deal with unanswered questions. It seemed that everyone was talking about the Laci Peterson case and theories bloomed, then multiplied like barnacles clinging to the rotting hull of a sunken ship.

Some of the first stories that began to circulate speculated that the woman's remains were headless, like the body of Evelyn Hernandez, and may have been missing some of the limbs. Those stories quickly turned to speculation that the corpses of several other area women missing for some time from the area were floating around in the water or mired at the bottom of the bay — without their heads.

If some of the gossip was correct and the head, and possibly the arms, was missing from the woman whose remains washed up in the Point Isabel area of the East Bay, Lee's reluctance to comment about dental records was significant. And if the hands or arms were missing, there would also be no chance of making a positive identification through fingerprints. But it was known that Laci had the small sunflower tattoo and if her left foot was recovered with the remains, the design might lead to her identification. Depending on what they had to work with, X-rays could also have been taken to pinpoint any broken bones from old mishaps, so the investigators could attempt to match the fractures with Laci — or someone else. Signs of an old fracture could also be used to eliminate Laci as the victim.

Police detectives and others working on the case weren't about to sit around on their hands, waiting for forensic pathologists to finish with all their work on the bodies or for laboratory tests to solve the twin mystery for them.

A secret witness had been helping them piece together a double murder case against Scott — a truck driver who had come forward with information that literally sank Scott's alibi, a source close to the case disclosed.

"A truck driver came forward to tell police that around 3:30 in the morning of Dec. 24, he was driving on a highway close to the marina area and saw a truck pulling an aluminum boat," the source revealed. "He was interested because he was thinking of buying a boat himself. He pulled up alongside, close enough to check the maker's name on the boat — Gamefisher. Some time later, the trucker saw a picture in the paper of Scott's truck and boat and recognized them from his Christmas Eve trip."

Shockingly, the driver had spotted Scott in the dead of night near the scene where Laci's body was disposed of — at the very time Scott claimed he was still at home with her.

Determined investigators also remained busy on another front after the bodies washed up on the beach, turning on their computers to scan missing persons lists from the bay area, then all of California. The remains were in such poor shape they didn't have much in the way of a physical description of the victim. Nevertheless, they combed meticulously through the names and physical descriptions of missing women who may have been about the age of the dead woman.

Meanwhile, after learning that bodies believed to be Laci and Conner had washed up on the shore of the bay, Sharon Rocha dialed Scott on his cell phone and asked that he fly from San Diego to help identify his wife. His icy demeanor chilled Laci's family and investigators.

"If Scott really cared for Laci and Conner, he would have been on the first plane to San Francisco," a source close to the family declared. "He would do everything possible to ease her family's suffering. Instead, the voice on the end of the phone was cold and distant. He didn't seem to show any emotion," the contact said.

Scott reportedly made some excuse about having to do a lot of things in San Diego. His shocking reaction deepened the suspicions that he had some awful secrets to hide.

Gruesome details were continuing to be uncovered by press snoops. The rumors about Laci's head being missing were correct. It was gone and her right arm, part of her left leg and her right foot were also missing. Pathologists were unable to determine if her body was chopped up to fit into a steel drum, which police were convinced she was stuffed into, or if the limbs and head became separated from the body through decomposition.

"You could see the bones of her rib cage and look right through the body and see the backbone," Sgt. Enos Johnson of the Richmond Police Department revealed.

Conner's body was also badly decomposed. Medical experts explained that the infant was expelled from his mother's body through a phenomenon known as "coffin birth," during which gases from the decomposing woman forced the child outside her womb. Police believe those gasses also blew open the drum containing her mutilated corpse.

Crabs and other sea creatures chewing on Laci's remains, along with normal underwater movement, eventually freed her from the concrete anchors and allowed her to float to the surface, authorities believed. Sources close to the case speculated that the head and legs were wired to weights, but during recent storms' tide surges and bodily gases that made her buoyant pulled Laci free, leaving some of her body parts behind. Investigators reportedly surmised that the ankle weights Scott was said to have bought with a credit card shortly before Laci's disappearance could have been a factor in the loss of parts of both of Laci's legs.

Famed coroner Dr. Cyril Wecht confided to reporters: "I think Laci was most probably strangled or suffocated." Once the mother was dead, little Conner would have lived no longer than 10 minutes, Wecht said.

Dr. Wecht has both a medical degree and a law degree, served for years as head of pathology at Pittsburgh's St. Francis Central Hospital and is regarded as one of the preeminent pathologists in the nation. He has performed autopsies on the famous and the powerful, including cult leader David Koresh, who died in the Branch Davidian conflagration near Waco, Texas, and the former commander in chief of the Pakistan Army. He also is noted for publicly airing controversial opinions on such notable deaths as President John F. Kennedy, U.S. Senator Robert Kennedy, Elvis Presley and Nicole Brown Simpson. When Wecht talks about cause of death in a high-profile murder case, people pay attention.

While police, forensic pathologists, DNA experts, other investigators and laboratory specialists were working to conclusively identify the bodies found on the beach, the prime suspect remained in Southern California, where he was occupied in behavior that could be considered extremely curious.

Scott was spending hundreds of dollars on survival gear — the kind of equipment that could have come in handy if he was planning to hide out in the rugged mountains of Mexico. Mexico's laws do not provide for capital punishment and the country won't give up accused killers to other countries without a stipulation that the death penalty will not be sought.

Scott bought the survival gear at the REI outdoors store on Copley Drive in San Diego and paid cash. Employees in the store said they suspected he was the husband of the missing woman who was dominating the news in California, but weren't sure until he filled out an application for REI club membership, which entitled him to a 10 percent discount.

"Yes, I am Scott Peterson," he boldly conceded, confidently smiling at the clerk who helped on him. Scott was arrogant in the way he said his name, the clerk later recalled. "He seemed to enjoy the notoriety."

The clerk added that during their discussion Scott said, "I recently came back from Mexico and I am going there again."

A large tent and a cover to shield it from the sun, a water purification system capable of making rancid water suitable for drinking and bathing, a camp stove, a sleeping bag, a tent chair, a compass and a large supply of dried and canned food were among the errant husband's purchases.

"Scott was well aware of the Mexican extradition laws as they applied to the death penalty," an investigator close to the case revealed. "He knew that even if he was eventually discovered hiding out, the authorities in Modesto would have to forgo asking for the death penalty to get Mexico to turn him over for prosecution."

While the troubled fertilizer salesman was taking care of business close to the Mexican border, the press temporarily lost track of him. Neither his lawyer nor members of his family was willing to reveal where he was. When Doug Ridenour talked with reporters on Thursday, April 17, the Modesto Police Department spokesman explained that Scott was not a suspect and authorities couldn't restrict his movements. Only a judge or the courts has the authority to restrict someone's Fourth Amendment rights (which protects people from unreasonable searches and seizures). Ridenour refused to say if police knew where Scott was.

Laci's dad, however, figured that his son-in-law's days as a free man were numbered and he told a Boston television reporter he thought it was only a matter of time before Scott was arrested and charged. "I just can't see Scott being out there free," he said. "That would just eat me up."

But even though Scott was spending most of his time in the old familiar stomping grounds around San Diego more than 350 miles from Modesto, he was neither out of sight or out of mind for the dogged homicide investigators from the San Joaquin Valley.

Police were sticking close to his trail. Detectives knew where he was and they were pretty sure they knew what he was up to.

Chapter 15

AN END TO THE CHASE

Good Friday, April 18, was a banner day in the nearly four-month-long investigation into the perplexing disappearance of the pregnant woman that was captivating a nation. Scott Peterson was placed under arrest on two counts of capital murder — one for the death of Laci and the other for the death of Conner.

A few hours later, California Attorney

General Bill Lockyer confirmed that the bodies recovered on the shore of San Francisco Bay were those of Laci and Conner. DNA tests were finalized and yielded positive identification on the mother and son.

"There is no question in our minds that the unidentified female is Laci Peterson and the unidentified fetus is the biological child of Laci and Scott Peterson," Lockyer announced at a nationally televised news conference in the bay area. The cause of death in both cases was still undetermined.

With the DNA identifications confirmed, the investigation was turned over to the Modesto Police Department. Those officials, accompanied by local officers, stopped Scott late Friday morning as he drove a Mercedes-Benz near the Torrey Pines Golf Course in La Jolla a few miles north of San Diego, only 30 miles from the Mexican border. Scott — who gave up his $25,000 membership at Modesto's Del Rio Country Club when other golfers got together and bought him out — was dressed for a day on the links in a white polo shirt and khaki shorts. He and his father, Lee, had signed up for an 8 o'clock tee time that morning.

Astonishingly, when Scott was arrested

and handcuffed, his naturally brown hair was freshly bleached strawberry blond and he had grown a goatee and moustache. He was also carrying $10,000 in cash.

Whether he was surprised at the arrest or not, Scott was aware that he was being trailed by police in unmarked cars. In the deliberately cocky manner he had adopted since becoming the subject of so much attention, he deliberately taunted his relentless pursuers, flaunting his freedom. Lockyer said he behaved like a "smartaleck," by driving up and down the freeway waving at the grimly determined officers on his tail. Scott even pulled his car over to the side of the road one time and walked back to the detectives to ask why they were following him, the state attorney general said.

At a news conference in Modesto, Police Chief Roy Wasden revealed that a team of investigators had been watching Scott for some time. They "felt like it was important and necessary a little after 11 this morning to make an arrest," he said. He indicated that there was concern about Scott making the short run from San Diego to Mexico if he learned that his wife and son were definitely identified through the DNA samples.

Homicide detectives moved quickly. "From documents police found in the car, it appeared Scott was headed to Mexico or Brazil," a source close to the case confided. The cash found in his possession added credence to that supposition.

Being arrested for murder is a sobering experience and Scott seemed to have lost his previous cockiness. He didn't resist as his hands were cuffed and he was helped into the back seat of a police vehicle for the long drive back to the Stanislaus County Jail in Modesto. When he was driven up to the jail about midnight, 13 hours after his arrest, a crowd of 200 people had gathered to jeer and hold up signs that read: "Murderer" and "Baby Killer." The news spread quickly and the street and walkways in front of and around the complex of government buildings were jammed with private citizens, reporters, TV trucks and equipment.

Inside the jail, Scott was expertly run through the booking process. It was a routine that the staff carried out almost 1,500 times every month. The new inmate was fingerprinted, posed for mug shots and issued a bright red jumpsuit that was the uniform for most of the inmates. Finally, he was led into a cell in the maximum security section of the jail and locked up. Scott and inmates in five other cells that made up the special tier could watch television on a set that was mounted on a wall in the outside hall.

The subdued young man didn't land in maximum security because he was believed to be more dangerous than other inmates, but because it was feared he was in danger of being harmed by them. The threat of violence from other inmates is a problem in most jails and prisons for people locked up for celebrity and high-profile crimes or other offenses that are considered to be especially heinous — such as murdering a pregnant woman who is carrying the accused perpetrator's own baby.

Other prisoners had already made threats against the newcomer. Three strikers especially, men who were facing life in prison because they were anticipating their third felony conviction, might figure they had nothing to lose by injuring or killing an inmate like Scott, who was accused of such a notorious crime. And once they moved into the general population of some California prison they could bask in their own dark celebrity, with respectful recognition among their own kind.

For the first few days after Scott's arrest,

he was held under safety watch, according to the *Modesto Bee*, which meant that deputies checked him out every 15 minutes instead of every half-hour, as they do for most inmates. In many other jails, corrections officers use a different term — "suicide watch." Being locked up for the first time in your life is a shattering experience and suicides are a grim fact of life in the nation's jails and prisons.

Other inmates typically locked in maximum security may include high-level escape risks, violent troublemakers, child molesters or killers and snitches. Even the country's toughest jails and prisons hold people who are considered by their fellow stick-up artists, serial rapists and murderers to be bottom feeders. For the time being, those were the kind of men who would be Scott's closest neighbors.

Stanislaus County Sheriff's Department spokeswoman Kelly Huston later told reporters in a briefing outside the jail that Scott was "rather quiet" and "very courteous" since being booked. He talked to his lawyer on Saturday night, she added. "Like many people who are in jail for the first time, he wants to know what's next."

While Scott impatiently cooled his heels in

his cramped five-by-nine-foot cell, Attorney General Lockyer publicly described the case against him as "a slam dunk." That comment infuriated Scott's parents, who remarked about what they considered to be the shoddy, unprofessional behavior of police and the harassment of their son. In an interview, Lee claimed police "just bungled this investigation from day one ... I'm feeling like I'm living in Nazi Germany or the Soviet Union. I'm just sick of this."

The possible political element of the attorney general's public intrusion into the sensational case wasn't lost on the California press, which was closely watching Lockyer as a probable Democratic candidate for Governor Gray Davis' job in 2006, when the next gubernatorial elections rolled around. Lockyer's sudden prominence also sparked comments from big-time Los Angeles defense attorney Mark Geragos, who had been holding a highly visible role himself as a television commentator and expert on the legal aspects of the case. Geragos told reporters that developments had clearly put Lockyer "in the post position for the governor's race."

Many other Californians had other motivations for feeling they should become involved — even if it was in the smallest way — to show their empathy with the murdered woman and her family.

On Easter Sunday, only two days after Scott's arrest, while Christians all over the world were celebrating a resurrection, many residents in Modesto made a sad pilgrimage to a forlorn green clapboard house in the La Loma neighborhood to remember and mourn two lives that were terribly wasted. They turned the lawn in front of the empty home on Covena Avenue into a makeshift memorial to the glowing expectant mother and the innocent baby boy so cruelly snuffed out by murder. Many of the mourners had lost their own babies, sisters and other loved ones to miscarriages, mishaps or violence.

In a constant procession, thousands of men, women and children stopped to grieve and to pray, leaving behind a brightly colored field of Easter eggs, bunny rabbits, balloons, butterflies and teddy bears. Sunday would have been Conner's first Easter — if he had been allowed to live.

Thousands of signs and notes, most of them handwritten, were also left behind. Some of the messages were touchingly sympathetic and loving. Others betrayed the frustration and anger of the authors. "May You Both Rest In Peace In God's Hands," one sign read. "Gone With The Angels To Heaven," said another. "Scott: God Knows And We Know You Did It!" a third mourner had written.

Ginnie Nevarez was one of the pilgrims who stopped by on that sad Sunday. She was pregnant. "I went to Downey High School here in Modesto with Laci," the 26-year-old explained as she clutched a bouquet of red roses and fought back tears. "I will always remember her laughing smile. She was always so happy. And now I'm having my baby and she's not able to have hers."

Monday morning, the day after Easter, Scott was arraigned before Superior Court Judge Nancy Ashley on twin counts of capital murder. District Attorney James Brazelton formally filed the murder charges only a few hours before, accusing Scott in separate counts of acting "intentionally, deliberately and with premeditation" in the slaying of his wife and the couple's unborn child. The documents didn't specify what the murder weapon was or the cause of death, but significantly they included the special circumstance stipulating multiple murder, meaning that the prosecution could seek the death penalty.

Even without the filing of a so-called special circumstance, Scott and his defense team had much to worry about. California is one of 29 states that authorize capital murder charges for the intentional killing of a fetus, making an exception only for abortions.

California expanded its old 1872 murder law in 1973, adding the words "or a fetus" so that with the alteration the statute read: "Murder is the unlawful killing of a human being, or a fetus, with malice aforethought." The refashioned law stipulates that the unborn victim must have progressed from the embryonic stage, about 6 to 8 weeks, to be considered a fetus. The 1973 alteration was a significant change that more than a quarter of a century later could potentially lead to Scott's own life ending in the death chamber at California's notorious old San Quentin Prison on the north shore of San Francisco Bay — overlooking the waters that finally yielded the pathetic bodies of Laci and baby Conner. In California, the condemned have a choice: lethal injection or the gas chamber.

As court officers prepared for the arraignment, the defendant was led inside, manacled with handcuffs and a belly chain.

He wore his standard jail issue red jumpsuit, which was open at the collar and showed the top of his white T-shirt. Several seats in the 56-seat courtroom were reserved for members of Scott's and Laci's families and others were set aside for the press. The few remaining spots available to the general public were awarded by lottery. Courthouse workers and lawyers milled around in the hall.

Security was rigid and carefully mapped out ahead of time. At 10 o'clock Sunday night, police blocked off 11th Street between H and I streets in front of the courthouse. News trucks were the only civilian vehicles allowed inside the cordon and they were directed to park across the street. Five additional sheriff's deputies were assigned to beef up the regular security screening staff at the entrance to the courthouse and to deal with the crowd gathered outside.

Scott had abruptly broken off with his lawyer, Kirk McAllister, and told the court he couldn't afford to hire his own attorney. Stanislaus County Public Defender Tim Bazar was appointed to lead his defense.

Some of Scott's fertilizer customers had said they didn't see much of him after the trouble over Laci's disappearance began and, although no one was saying much about his personal finances, it appeared they weren't in very good shape. He was apparently strapped for money when he traded Laci's Range Rover in on the Dodge Ram, leading to such an outburst of criticism that used car dealer Doug Roberts gave the SUV back to her family and absorbed the loss. Scott also talked to at least three title companies about selling the house, according to the *Modesto Bee*, which could have been another indication that he was desperately short on funds.

The hearing was brief and when asked for his plea, Scott declared in a voice that was firm and unwavering: "I am not guilty!"

On April 27, a week after the outpouring of sympathy by friends and strangers in front of the empty Peterson home on Covena Avenue, an overflowing crowd of mourners crammed into the First Baptist Church in Modesto for a memorial service arranged for Laci's family and others who loved her. They were there to remember Laci and to celebrate her life — and the life that little Conner might have lived. Laci would have turned 28 years old that day.

The charming woman with the contagious smile was there in spirit, but her recovered remains and those of Conner were still held in the morgue at the Contra Costa Coroner's Office in Martinez.

Every pew in the main worship hall of the big church at the corner of 12th and M streets was filled, accommodating 1,900 people. Another 1,200 mourners watched on closed circuit TV from one room that held 800 people and another held 400.

On a huge stage a 120-voice choir, resplendent in white gowns, was flanked by a profusion of red, pink and white flower arrangements. A large picture of Laci, flashing her trademark dimpled smile, was displayed. Significantly, for the young woman whose college major was ornamental horticulture and who so loved growing things, there was also a mini-jungle of fresh, live plants.

Laci's family was escorted solemnly inside five minutes before the services began. Dennis Rocha wiped at tears that welled from his red-rimmed eyes as he walked in carrying a bouquet. All the family members looked exhausted and drained as they prepared for one more test of their strength and emotions. Laci's brother Brent was the only family member who spoke to the assemblage. "Today is a good day," he said. "Today is Laci's birthday. All of us are given an opportunity to remember Laci and Conner. Laci would be very grateful and just astounded that she would get this kind of attention. I think with all of us here, we're sending a powerful message."

Brent recalled that at his grandmother's funeral three years ago, Laci told him that when she died, "I don't want people to be missing me. I want people to be happy."

It was agonizingly difficult to carry out her wishes, but her friends and relatives outside the immediately family tried their best. And they managed to bring some subdued chuckles when they shared anecdotes about Laci's effervescent pixie charm and spirited antics while she was growing up.

An important element of the moving service was a video tribute to Laci that traced her life from childhood through her college years to her pregnancy. Many mourners found themselves smiling through their tears as pictures of the tiny girl who became a woman with a 10-gallon grin were flashed on two huge video screens, rekindling fond memories of good times and shared love. There were even wedding pictures, but like others taken after her marriage, every image of Scott had been judiciously edited out. The service was concluded with the playing of Van Morrison's *Brown Eyed Girl*. The tune was a favorite of Laci's.

Scott missed the service, as he had missed candlelight vigils during the frantic search for his pregnant wife. Inmates of the Stanislaus County Jail are sometimes permitted to attend funerals and memorial services, but requests are handled on a case-by-case basis. The jail commander usually makes the decisions, but Sheriff Les Weidman has the final word. Scott prudently didn't ask to attend. It was obvious that his presence would be too unsettling and would only add to the family's grief. Amber was invited, but also decided not to attend because she was concerned about media attention and becoming a distraction that would interfere with the purpose of the memorial. In San Diego, the Petersons also took a pass.

The accused double murderer would remain exactly where he was for quite a while. Certainly for months, and possibly for years, the Stanislaus County Jail would be his home. His life would be controlled by strangers and he would have long hours behind steel bars to silently ponder his fate.

There wasn't much to look forward to that promised even the smallest break in the boredom. Three meals were delivered to his cell every day, he could read books delivered daily on a cart by a correctional officer and he was allowed to make collect telephone calls, which authorities had the right to monitor.

Twice a week Scott was led to the roof of the four-story jail and allowed to work out for 90 minutes in an exercise area that was fenced off and topped with rolls of barbed wire. The exercise area had a basketball hoop, but it wasn't fancy. There wasn't even so much as a putting green for the former golf scholarship winner.

As a maximum-security inmate, two deputies always escorted Scott when he was outside his cell — to and from court appearances, during his every-other-day showers and while he exercised. They were his constant shadows.

The jail wasn't escape proof — an inmate or two had managed to break out since it was opened in August 1955 — and even some of the nation's toughest lockups, such as San Quentin and the former federal prison at Alcatraz, have lost an occasional prisoner. But the corrections staff at the Stanislaus

County Jail was competent and professional and it was about as secure as a jail can be.

The most frequent breaks in Scott's dreary routine were meetings with his legal counsel, held in a private room provided at the jail for inmates to talk with their attorneys. Scott was also allowed two family visits every week. He could have agreed to interviews with the press, but by the time he landed behind bars he was securely "lawyered up" and wasn't talking with reporters.

The prosecution and the defense were busy putting together their teams for a sensational case that courthouse regulars were already speculating might take three to five years to bring to trial. That amount of time to prepare for a final courtroom face-off wasn't unique for California and trials themselves were known to sometimes last years. The way things were shaping up, the combined legal process for the pretrial procedures and the trial in Scott's case was going to be one of the long ones.

District Attorney Brazelton and other senior members of his staff had talked about the death penalty among themselves and met with members of Laci's family to tap their feelings on capital punishment. That verdict, at least, was in — Brazelton revealed that Scott would be put on trial for his life. The prosecution was seeking the death penalty.

Thousands of pages of police and other reports were being gathered and organized by the prosecutors. Several bulging files of documents were already in the hands of deputy public defenders and more were being prepared to be turned over as part of the process known as "discovery" — which helps cut down on Perry Mason style courtroom surprises when a case has finally gone to trial.

But as the still-developing prosecution and defense teams formed and began digging in for the long run, some startling surprises were lurking just around the corner.

Chapter 16

THE COURTS

Scott's ultimate fate will be decided in the Stanislaus County Courthouse, an imposing four-story structure that is part of a landmark complex of buildings that take up a full square block in downtown Modesto and are devoted to complicated workings of the legal justice system.

Aside from the baleful business that frequently takes place inside, the complex located between 11th and 12th streets from H to I streets is attractive and even offers a touch of local history to casual visitors who care enough to stop at a gurgling fountain that provides the base for a 7-foot-tall statue of a 19th century American Indian.

Located at the corner of 11th and I streets, Mistlin Fountain is fronted by a plaque that identifies the Indian, dressed in a loincloth with a bow in his left hand and a quill of six arrows slung across his right shoulder, as Chief Estanislao.

The county's name is traced to the Indian chief, not for a famous early explorer, general or wealthy merchant from Poland, Czechoslovakia or some other Eastern European country, as many strangers to the area assume. The word "Stanislaus" is a corruption of Estanislao, the baptismal name of the mission-educated renegade Indian who led a band of braves in a series of battles against Mexican troops before he was finally defeated in 1826 by General Mariano G. Vallejo. For a while, one of the major streams in the area was called the Rio Estanislao, but it was later changed to the Stanislao River, and the name was later adopted for Stanislaus County.

Inside the pale yellow courthouse, the men and women who were preparing to do battle over Scott's fate were not concerned with 200-year-old history, but with making new local legal history during the most sensational trial ever to come down the pike in Modesto. There were already some surprising new players.

Mark Geragos, the high-profile, media-smart Los Angeles lawyer who had so much to say about the Peterson case on *Larry King Live* and other television talk shows was taking over the defense and Tim Bazar and a co-counsel with the public defender's office were bowing out. That meant a huge savings of money for local taxpayers who were already deeply in hock for hundreds of thousands of dollars spent on the investigation and the initial stages of the court proceedings.

Scott's faithful parents would be paying the bill for the defense, which some experts expected to reach $1 million or more for what was anticipated as years of weary, time-consuming and expensive legal wrangling. Stanislaus County was still on the hook for the prosecution costs.

In a Superior Court hearing, Judge Al Girolami, who had taken over the criminal case, at least for the time being, permitted the change of counsel after inquiring about who was going to be paying the bills. "I was retained by Mr. Peterson's family," Geragos replied. Scott responded in the affirmative when the judge asked if he agreed to the change.

Lee and Jackie Peterson were the owners of a successful business, San Diego Packing and Crating, but that kind of an expenditure for a couple who was already grandparents was seen by some observers as a tremendous sacrifice. The couple nevertheless believed in their son from the beginning and were fiercely determined to stick it out and see him through the remainder of the ordeal.

Big-time criminal defense lawyers aren't known for announcing their fee arrangements, but seasoned courtroom warriors like Geragos don't come cheap. And he was still putting together a high-priced team of co-counsels and assistants.

Scott and Geragos were locked in a five-hour conference at the jail while Laci's family and friends mourned and celebrated her life at the Sunday memorial in the First Baptist Church. Scott and the lawyer were talking before the memorial started and they were still talking long after it ended.

Lawyering was the ethnic Armenian Geragos' family business and his father and a brother were also attorneys. Scott's new

attorney graduated from Loyola Law School
in 1982 before joining Geragos & Geragos,
his father's Los Angeles law firm. He learned
quickly and by the time he took over Scott's
case he had accumulated a dazzling résumé.
The Los Angeles attorney was known for
representing such high-profile clients as
Hollywood actress Winona Ryder in her
shoplifting trial; U.S. Congressman Gary
Condit in the Chandra Levy investigation;
President Bill Clinton's younger brother,
Roger, and the elder Clinton's friend Susan
McDougal of Whitewater fame. Susan drew
national headlines in a sensational
California proceeding before she was convicted of theft and obstruction of justice in
an unrelated case.

Geragos moved quickly to get his client out
of the red jail uniform and into civilian
clothes for hearings and other proceedings
he was expected to attend. Lawyers hate
having their clients shuffle into court in
ankle cuffs, handcuffs, belly chains and a
bright red jail uniform because it makes
them look like criminals. The judge agreed
that because of the massive publicity in the
case, too many people viewing pictures of
Scott in the jumpsuit and shackles might be

prejudicial to potential jurors. Girolami agreed to permit the defendant to skip the shackles and wear civilian clothes to the hearings.

Scott soon had another prominent lawyer on his team who was especially well-known in Modesto. His former counsel, Kirk McAllister, came back on board. McAllister's shock of snow-white hair made him look like he could be someone's kindly old grandfather, but the crusty courtroom veteran was always focused, had a steel-trap mind and a formidable reputation for getting the job done.

Scott was well-represented and if he didn't get a fair trial it seemed unlikely that it would be because his lawyers didn't know their way around in a courtroom.

The district attorney also formed the core of his team. Brazelton assigned two of his most experienced prosecutors — senior district attorneys Rick Distaso and David Harris — to handle the state's case.

Groundwork had already been laid by McAllister's so-called "parallel investigation" for what some observers suspected might become the strategy to be adopted for Scott's defense. Geragos was impressed after reading reports on the probe, which is said to have pinpointed mysterious strangers seen in the La Loma neighborhood shortly before Laci vanished.

A plethora of other theories were also popping up in the press or discussed at hair salons, barbershops and busy watering holes — wherever people gathered and the talk turned to Laci — blaming the ghastly crime on everyone from bumbling burglars to sinister blood cultists or ruthless Satanists driven by hunger for innocent babies to sacrifice to the Prince of Evil. Theories ranged from the outrageous to the asinine.

But speculation that Laci and Conner may have been kidnapped for human sacrifice was given new fuel when *Fox News* reported that Laci's body was grossly mutilated by her killer, who cut off her head and removed internal body parts. The chilling report was aired amid news that pathologists with the Contra Costa County Coroner's Office had completed the autopsies on the mother and child. The results were immediately sealed by Judge Al Girolami in Modesto. The judge also ordered the remains to stay at the coroner's office for the time being. It was unknown when Laci's grieving family would finally be allowed to lay their loved ones to rest.

Fox quoted a source on Scott's legal team as describing the condition of Laci's corpse as "horrendous" — "awful, awful, awful." The absence or near absence of blood found in the Peterson home led to speculation that Laci may have been carved up in the bathtub.

The television news report also indicated that pathologists were unsuccessful in efforts to determine the cause of death. That was probably behind a renewed effort to recover evidence from San Francisco Bay. The weekend after it was learned that the autopsy report was issued, divers and others resumed their search of the waters near the Berkeley Marina. Police Lieutenant Ridenour left a recorded message at the Modesto Police Department, disclosing that various law enforcement agencies and private firms were cooperating in the renewed search effort.

With grisly new revelations continuing to dominate news about Laci, the public horror over the ghastly fate of the pregnant woman and her unborn baby was growing, not subsiding, and the work of Geragos and other members of Scott's legal team was cut out for them.

Outside the courtroom, one of the media-savvy lawyer's main tasks was reshaping and rebuilding Scott's reputation. At the time Geragos agreed to defend Scott, the embattled fertilizer salesman may well have been the most widely hated man in America. It promised to be a long time before jury selection began. But when the jury venue was at last summoned, Geragos wanted potential panelists to see a different Scott Peterson than the heartless monster who was being depicted in the press.

Geragos publicly vowed to clear his client and find the person who really killed Laci and her son. Some skeptical observers suggested that perhaps they should team up with ex-football great O.J. Simpson, who also vowed to run down the real killer of his wife Nicole, following his acquittal in another sensational California murder trial.

The prospect is a long way down the road, but if Scott is convicted of capital murder and sentenced to death, he will be locked up with real killers much like the dope dealers and hit men O.J.'s lawyers alluded to. Some of the death row inmates are even worse.

Scott's neighbors on death row would be people like homicidal pedophile Richard Davis and "Nightstalker" Richard Ramirez.

Davis is the savage and serial sex offender who in 1983 kidnapped Polly Hannah Klaas from her bedroom at knifepoint during a slumber party in her home, then strangled her. Davis had a criminal rap sheet 13 pages long and Polly's slaying coupled with another notorious crime that occurred about the same time led to adoption of California's tough "three strikes" law. Boiled down to laymen's terms, the law mandates a 25 years to life term in prison for a third felony conviction. If "three strikes" had already been the law in 1983 when Davis began stalking Polly, he would still have been behind bars for earlier crimes. Instead, the girl died a horrible death and Davis went to death row.

Ramirez was a crazed, Satan-loving cocaine fiend when he raged through suburban Los Angeles and San Francisco in the early 1980s, breaking into homes, shooting the men and then raping and killing the women. His two-year reign of terror claimed the lives of 14 people and earned him a nickname as "The Nightstalker." Outrageously, his gruesome notoriety and sexual magnetism resulted in dozens of marriage proposals from serial killer groupies and he eventually selected one of the eager candidates to become his bride — and tied the knot while he was on death row.

According to experienced correctional authorities, it's only a matter of time before Scott can expect to begin receiving his own fan letters and marriage proposals from women seeking to share his dark celebrity and bask in his notoriety.

But a possible trip to San Quentin's crowded death row is years in the future for Scott, if it ever occurs at all. In the meantime, he can expect to remain securely locked in the Stanislaus County Jail. He can also anticipate spending hundreds of hours conferring with his attorneys or observing them at work in the courtroom during innumerable hearings and other legal proceedings.

It is a dark outlook for a young man known for his love of the outdoors — but well-deserved if guilty of this heinous crime.

Conclusion

LACI'S LEGACY

The frustrating vagaries and capricious failings of California's criminal justice system makes it a certainty that the emotional wounds inflicted on the people who love Laci — and those who love Scott — will continue to be rubbed raw for years.

Laci's fear and suffering and the lost opportunities for little Conner will be painfully recalled every time there's a major court hearing, throughout the long months of an anticipated lengthy murder trial — and if Scott is convicted and sentenced to be executed — during innumerable and emotionally exhausting years of death row appeals.

It was late in 1996, almost exactly three years after Richard Davis' arrest for the murder of Polly Klaas, before he was finally convicted and sentenced. He has already been on death row for seven years. California has an abysmal record of carrying out the mandate of the people and executing its most vicious criminals, and death row at San Quentin is crammed with more than 600 inmates. Many of the condemned men have been there much longer than Davis.

Even if Scott joins their dismal ranks, there is every reason to believe that he will outlive many of the people who were close to Laci, were involved in the investigation or joined in the search.

But the world goes on and the bright-eyed, high-spirited and loving woman who helped make it a better place for her devoted circle of family and friends will be remembered for other things.

Laci was an animal lover and she would have been pleased to know that McKenzie and her prized pair of Siamese-mix cats were resettled in new homes, where they will be treasured and well cared for.

McKenzic, as reported by the *Modesto Bee*, is living with one of Scott's siblings — and despite the painful break with the Rochas after his deception was revealed — the Petersons obviously loved Laci, too. The handsome, friendly golden retriever will be a reminder of happier days.

Laci's cats, Siam and Gracie, were seriously spooked by all the commotion and it took a while for her friends to coax them from bushes outside the house with food and capture them in wicker baskets. After a checkup by a veterinarian, they were turned over to one of Laci's closest friends, Stacey Boyers, who became their new mom.

In addition to her well-known love of animals, Laci may yet leave another important legacy behind, one that Conner is a part of.

Laci's family — parents, stepfather and siblings — joined together to publicly support legislation introduced in the U.S. Congress to make the killing of a fetus a federal crime.

"As the family of Laci Peterson and her unborn son, Conner, this bill is very close to our hearts," they declared in a letter of support disclosed on Capitol Hill. "We have not only lost our future with our daughter and sister, but with our grandson and nephew as well."

U.S. Representative Melissa Hart, who successfully sponsored a similar bill while she was in the Pennsylvania state legislature, introduced the new federal measure in Congress. She identified the bill as "the Unborn Victims of Violence Act — or "Laci and Conner's Law."